ELEVEN
BRITISH POETS

ELEVEN
BRITISH POETS

AN ANTHOLOGY
EDITED BY
Michael Schmidt

ROUTLEDGE
LONDON AND NEW YORK

First published in 1980 by
Methuen & Co. Ltd
Reprinted 1987
This anthology © Methuen & Co. Ltd
Reprinted 1988, 1990
by Routledge
11 New Fetter Lane,
London EC4P 4EE
29 West 35th Street,
New York NY 10001

Printed in Great Britain at the
University Press, Cambridge

British Library Cataloguing in Publication Data

Eleven British poets.
1. English poetry – 20th century
I. Schmidt, Michael
821'.9'1208   PR1225   80–49955

ISBN 0–415–03993–2 Pbk
(University paperbacks)

FOR
HELEN
LEFROY

Contents

Acknowledgements xiii
Introduction 1

R. S. Thomas 9

A Peasant	10
Song for Gwydion	11
Welsh Landscape	11
The Village	12
Taliesin 1952	12
In a Country Church	13
The Return	13
Bread	14
Genealogy	14
Here	15
The Moor	16
The Belfry	16
In Church	17
Concession	17
Tenancies	18
Petition	18
Period	19
Pavane	19
Making	20
Emerging	20
The Casualty	21
The Calling	22
Pilgrimages	23

C. H. Sisson 25

In the Hills	26
The Un-red Deer	27
Christmas at the Greyhound	27
The Temple	27
Good-Day, Citizen	28
A Letter to John Donne	28

from Metamorphoses 30
Homo Sapiens is of No Importance 31
The Recollection 32
The Person 34
Evening 34
The Usk 35
Sumptuary Laws 37
In Spring-Time 37
Gardening 38
Marcus Aurelius 38
Over the Wall 39
Swimming the Horses 41
Est in Conspectu Tenedos 41
Narcissus 42
Moon-Rise 43
The Red Admiral 44
Autumn Poems 45
In Flood 46

W. S. GRAHAM 51

O Gentle Queen of the Afternoon 52
Let Me Measure My Prayer with Sleep 53
Gigha 54
To My Brother 54
Listen Put On Morning 55
Yours Truly 56
The Thermal Stair 57
Imagine a Forest 59
Johann Joachim Quantz's Five Lessons 61
How are the Children Robin 64
To My Wife at Midnight 64

DONALD DAVIE 70

Poem as Abstract 71
Remembering the 'Thirties 72
Time Passing, Beloved 74
Dream Forest 74
The Wearing of the Green 75
A Winter Talent 76
Heigh-ho on a Winter Afternoon 76
With the Grain 77
A Lily at Noon 79

CONTENTS

Rodez	80
July, 1964	81
January	81
A Winter Landscape near Ely	82
Epistle. To Enrique Caracciolo Trejo	83
Rousseau in His Day	84
Portland	85
Grudging Respect	85
The Fountain of Cyane	86

PHILIP LARKIN 94

Wedding-Wind	95
Next, Please	96
Going	97
Wants	97
Church Going	98
I Remember, I Remember	99
At Grass	100
Here	101
Mr Bleaney	102
Nothing To Be Said	103
Toads Revisited	104
Days	105
Ambulances	105
An Arundel Tomb	106
The Old Fools	107
High Windows	109
How Distant	109
Sad Steps	110
The Explosion	111

ELIZABETH JENNINGS 113

The Island	114
In the Night	115
Ghosts	115
Choices	116
Fountain	117
Song for a Birth or a Death	118
My Grandmother	118
The Resurrection	119
Night Garden of the Asylum	120
The Animals' Arrival	120

✓ Light   121
✓ A Quartet   121
✓ I Feel   122
✓ Rembrandt's Late Self-Portraits   122
✓ Into the Hour   123
✓ An Answer to Odd Advice   124
✓ Goldfinch   124
✓ Watcher   125
✓ Thought and Feeling   125
✓ On its Own   126

CHARLES TOMLINSON   127

Tramontana at Lerici   128
Paring the Apple   129
More Foreign Cities   130
At Holwell Farm   130
The Picture of J.T. in a Prospect of Stone 131
The Snow Fences   132
Swimming Chenango Lake   134
Prometheus   135
Against Extremity   136
The Fox Gallery   137
Of Beginning Light   138
In Memoriam Thomas Hardy   138
The Marl Pits   139
After a Death   139
For Danton   141
In Arden   142

THOM GUNN   146

A Mirror for Poets   147
On The Move   148
To Yvor Winters, 1955   150
In Santa Maria del Popolo   151
Innocence   152
Considering the Snail   152
My Sad Captains   153
Touch   154
Epitaph for Anton Schmidt   155
Rites of Passage   156
The Garden of the Gods   157
Diagrams   158

Iron Landscapes (and the Statue of Liberty) 158
Thomas Bewick 159
Autobiography 160

TED HUGHES 164

The Thought-Fox 165
The Jaguar 166
The Horses 167
Wind 168
October Dawn 169
Six Young Men 170
Hawk Roosting 171
View Of A Pig 172
Thrushes 173
Her Husband 174
The Green Wolf 174
Out 175
Kafka 177
Full Moon and Little Frieda 177
Wodwo 178
Examination at the Womb-door 179
Crow Alights 179
Crow and the Birds 180
Crow's Last Stand 181
Apple Dumps 181
The River in March 182

GEOFFREY HILL 185

Genesis 186
Merlin 188
The White Ship 188
Doctor Faustus 189
To the (Supposed) Patron 190
Ovid in the Third Reich 191
September Song 191
Four Poems Regarding the Endurance of Poets 192
from The Songbook of Sebastian Arrurruz 194
The Pentecost Castle 196
Two Chorale-Preludes 202

SEAMUS HEANEY   206

Digging   207
The Diviner   208
Personal Helicon   209
The Salmon Fisher to the Salmon   209
The Forge   210
The Peninsula   210
Fodder   211
Servant Boy   212
The Wool Trade   212
The Tollund Man   213
May   215
Westering   215
Mossbawn: Two Poems in Dedication   217
Punishment   218
Exposure   219
After a Killing   221
Leavings   221

Index of first lines   225

Acknowledgements

The editor and publisher would like to thank the following for permission to reproduce copyright material:

Granada Publishing Ltd for 'A Peasant', 'Song for Gwydion', 'Welsh Landscape', 'The Village', 'Taliesin 1952', 'In a Country Church', 'The Return' from *Song at the Year's Turning*, 'Bread' from *Poetry for Supper*, 'Genealogy' and 'Here' from *Tares*, 'The Moor', 'The Belfry' and 'In Church' from *Pietà*, 'Concession' and 'Tenancies' from *Not That He Brought Flowers*, and Macmillan, London and Basingstoke, for 'Petition', 'Period', 'Pavane' and 'Making' from *H'm*, 'Emerging', 'The Casualty' and 'The Calling' from *Laboratories of the Spirit*, and 'Pilgrimages' from *Frequencies*, all by R. S. Thomas; Carcanet New Press Ltd for 'Narcissus', 'Moon-Rise', 'The Red Admiral', 'Autumn Poems' and 'In Flood' from *Exactions*, 'In the Hills', 'The Un-red Deer', 'Christmas at the Greyhound', 'The Temple', 'Good-Day, Citizen', 'A Letter to John Donne', 28 lines from 'Metamorphoses', 'Homo Sapiens is of No Importance', 'The Recollection', 'The Person', 'Evening', 'The Usk', 'Sumptuary Laws' and 'In Spring-Time' from *In The Trojan Ditch: Collected Poems and Selected Translations*, and 'Gardening', 'Marcus Aurelius', 'Over the Wall', 'Swimming the Horses' and 'Est in Conspectu Tenedos' from *Anchises*, all by C. H. Sisson; W. S. Graham for 'O Gentle Queen of the Afternoon' and 'Let Me Measure My Prayer with Sleep' from *Cage Without Grievance*, 'Gigha', 'To My Brother' and 'Listen Put On Morning' from *The White Threshold*, 'Yours Truly' and 'The Thermal Stair' from *Malcolm Mooney's Land*, 'Imagine a Forest', 'Johann Joachim Quantz's Five Lessons' and 'How are the Children Robin' from *Implements In Their Places*, and 'To My Wife at Midnight' from *W. S. Graham Collected Poems*

Arden' from *The Shaft* (© Charles Tomlinson 1978), all by Charles Tomlinson; Faber and Faber Ltd for 'A Mirror for Poets' from *Fighting Terms*, 'On The Move' and 'To Yvor Winters, 1955' from *The Sense Of Movement*, and 'Touch' and 'Epitaph for Anton Schmidt' from *Touch*, and Faber and Faber Ltd and Farrar, Straus and Giroux, Inc. for 'In Santa Maria del Popolo', 'Innocence', 'Considering the Snail' and 'My Sad Captains' from *My Sad Captains*, and 'Rites of Passage' and 'The Garden of the Gods' from *Moly* (the last six poems are available in the USA in *Moly and My Sad Captains* © Thom Gunn 1961, 1971 and 1973), and 'Diagrams', 'Iron Landscapes (and the Statue of Liberty)', 'Thomas Bewick' and 'Autobiography' from *Jack Straw's Castle* (© Thom Gunn 1971, 1973, 1974, 1975, 1976), all by Thom Gunn; Faber and Faber Ltd and Harper and Row, Publishers, Inc. for 'The Thought-Fox' (this poem originally appeared in the USA in *The New Yorker*), 'The Jaguar', 'The Horses' and 'Wind' (© Ted Hughes 1956), 'October Dawn' and 'Six Young Men' from *The Hawk in the Rain* (© Ted Hughes 1957), 'Hawk Roosting' (© Ted Hughes 1959), 'View Of A Pig' (© Ted Hughes 1960) and 'Thrushes' (© Ted Hughes 1959) from *Lupercal*, 'Her Husband' (© Ted Hughes 1961), 'The Green Wolf' (© Ted Hughes 1962), 'Out' (© Ted Hughes 1967), 'Kafka' (© Ted Hughes 1966), 'Full Moon and Little Frieda' (© Ted Hughes 1967) and 'Wodwo' (© Ted Hughes 1962) from *Wodwo*, (the last fifteen poems are available in the USA in *Ted Hughes Selected Poems 1957–1967*), and 'Examination at the Womb-door', 'Crow Alights', 'Crow and the Birds' and 'Crow's Last Stand' from *Crow* (© Ted Hughes 1971), Faber and Faber Ltd and Ted Hughes for 'Apple Dumps' from *Season Songs*, and Faber and Faber Ltd and Viking Penguin, Inc. for 'The River in March' from *Season Songs*, all by Ted Hughes; André Deutsch Ltd and Dufour Editions, Inc., Chester Springs, PA 19425, for 'Ovid in the Third Reich', 'September Song', 'Four Poems Regarding the Endurance of Poets' and 55 lines from 'The Songbook of Sebastian Arrurruz' from *King Log* (1968), and André Deutsch and Houghton Mifflin Company for 'Genesis', 'Merlin', 'The White Ship', 'Doctor Faustus', 'To the (Supposed) Patron' from *For the Unfallen: Poems 1952–1958*, and 'The Pentecost Castle' and 'Two Chorale-Preludes' from *Tenebrae*, all by Geoffrey Hill (the last seven poems are available in the USA in *Somewhere is Such a Kingdom: Poems 1952–1971* (© Geoffrey Hill 1975); Faber and Faber Ltd for 'Digging', 'The Diviner' and 'Personal Helicon' from *Death of a Naturalist*, and 'The Salmon Fisher to the Salmon', 'The Forge' and 'The Peninsula' from *Door Into The Dark*, Faber and Faber Ltd and Oxford University Press, Inc. for 'Fodder', 'Servant Boy', 'The Wool Trade', 'The Tollund Man', 'May' and 'Westering' from

Wintering Out (© Seamus Heaney 1972), and 'Mossbawn: Two Poems in Dedication', 'Punishment' and 'Exposure' from *North* (© Seamus Heaney 1975), and Faber and Faber Ltd and Farrar, Straus and Giroux, Inc. for 'After a Killing' and 'Leavings' from *Field Work* (© Seamus Heaney 1979), all by Seamus Heaney.

The editor is grateful to Claire Harman Schmidt for her valuable help in preparing this book.

Introduction

One of the best-known poems of the Second World War is Keith Douglas's 'How to Kill'. It includes the lines:

> Now in my dial of glass appears
> the soldier who is going to die.
> He smiles and moves about in ways
> his mother knows, habits of his.
> The wires touch his face: I cry
> NOW. Death, like a familiar, hears
>
> and look, has made a man of dust
> of a man of flesh. This sorcery
> I do. Being damned, I am amused
> to see the centre of love diffused
> and the waves of love travel into vacancy.
> How easy it is to make a ghost.

Here modern technology becomes brutal sorcery, the speaker of the poem is like Dr Faustus, the terms he uses those of the contract which bound that medieval German doctor to his damnation. Mechanized warfare and its effects on individual conscience and moral sensibility have seldom been so effectively evoked in verse. The poem is seemingly conventional. It has four six-line stanzas rhymed *abccba*. But the form itself, with that uneasy couplet at the heart and the *a* rhymes so separated as to be almost dispersed, is oddly exploded. The poet's attitude to his line-endings, his forceful spoken use of the enjambement, his avoidance of the natural emphases of the stanza, are a further element in the poem's powerful originality.

  Implicitly and explicitly the experiences of the Second World War, the bomb and of the Nazi and Soviet death-camps have haunted European writing, and British poetry of the post-war years is no exception. It has registered the war itself, its specific aftermath, its human and social consequences. Recent history has illuminated the destructive potential of human nature assisted by technology and ideology, changing our attitudes to the past and future as well as the present. Societies have altered, and language too speaks differently.

Keith Douglas left a mark on several of the poets included in this anthology. Ted Hughes edited a selection of his verse; in the introduction he noted that Douglas 'invented a style that seems to be able to deal poetically with whatever it comes up against. . . . It is a language for the whole mind, at its most wakeful, and in all situations'. We can trace direct debts to Douglas's poetry in some of Hughes's work. Charles Tomlinson and Geoffrey Hill are not untouched by this astonishingly complete poet who was killed in France in his twenty-fourth year. It is Douglas who made the now famous comment and prophecy:

> The soldiers have not found anything new to say. Their experience they will not forget easily, and it seems to me that the whole body of English war poetry of this war, civil and military, will be created after the war is over.

An over-statement, no doubt – but this anthology does not contradict it. Some of the best poetry of recent years considers the transformation in our sense of human nature, of history and of language which the war catalysed. Many poems approach the same theme that 'How to Kill' does, attempting a form of statement which reveals the pure, amoral action as it is conceived and carried out in a fully articulate, specifically Western consciousness, a consciousness which uses a language instinct with traditional values as if ignorant of those values, of the language's overtones and history. The speaker's consciousness is bared of human passion and response: his eye wonders and rejoices in a moral waste. The poet (as opposed to the speaker of the poem) trusts his reader to hear the qualifying irony of the historical language. If for Wilfred Owen the 'poetry is in the pity', for Keith Douglas and some of those who have valued his work the poetry is in the pitilessness. Douglas is not a suasive rhetorician but a witness to a cold reality. He accommodates what, in the 1920s, his eye on Swift, Edgell Rickword characterized as the 'negative emotions'. R. S. Thomas, clergyman and poet, writes:

> One thing I have asked
> Of the disposer of the issues
> Of life: that truth should defer
> To beauty. It was not granted.

The best modern poetry is consoling in its courage and honesty, not in any factitious sentiments it generates.

Part of the force of Douglas's poetry is that – unlike Owen's – it is not elegiac or overtly didactic. It accepts and portrays the given world; the moral comment is implicit in the terms of evocation. Douglas does not season with conventional spices the dish he serves us. He has extended poetry into one of the extreme areas of modern experience. Yet he penetrates that extreme area without hysteria – as it were dispassionately. That is the wonder of his verse: it is the world which is extreme, the strategy for survival and for witness is a kind of neutrality (but not passivity). How unlike this is to the fashionable 'extremist' verse of the 1960s, the verse of the lesser members of the 'confessional' school which demands that we credit the distortions of mental illness and private anguish, that we dwell upon effects rather than causes, upon the subject of experience rather than the experience itself. For Douglas such a procedure was unthinkable. His words bear their old meanings into new and given contexts. These contexts focus the words, and the words give weight to the contexts, even perhaps beyond the poet's intention: 'Words are my instruments but not my servants'. As the horrific experience of warfare receded, there came time for elegy, a lament for the particular and the general losses. Elegy, and the attempt to redefine the areas of possible poetic activity, have characterized post-war verse. The formal, thematic and moral variety attest to the uncertainty abroad, the failure of a consensus to form or re-form, and the isolated state of individual writers even within those short-lived 'movements' which journalists detect and try to define.

Whatever the truth of Douglas's prophecy, it is undeniable that the poems included in this anthology in several respects differ from those composed before the war: themes, tones, registers and forms, over and above the obvious modernity of some of their imagery, belong to the latter half of the twentieth century. They witness to a change in the language, in the culture and in the society. The change began before the First World War. It became unavoidable after the Second.

*

The earliest poems printed here pre-date Douglas's 'How to Kill'. The most recent were written in 1979. Poems from four decades, then; and poets from three. The perspectives are rather longer than the anthologist of contemporary verse is normally allowed and the number of poets is relatively small. The book is not intended to mirror a period; representative anthologies inevitably carry the burden of the mediocre of the age. It is, however, intended to bear witness to a living tradition, that tradition which made it possible for T. S.

Eliot to accommodate the 'Unreal City' in verse, for Ezra Pound to acclimatize Propertius in this century, and for Edward Thomas and Isaac Rosenberg to break their voices free of fashion and convention and speak for themselves. It is the tradition which extends the language of poetry by making it include new or newly apprehended experience. It extends poetry largely by virtue of its clear continuity with the past. None of the poets here is less than deeply acquainted with English and some European and classical literature. They are learned with the tact to know where their particular roots lie in the past. As Sainte-Beuve wrote, 'the first condition of taste, after obtaining knowledge of all, lies not in continual travel, but in rest and cessation from wandering'. Each of these poets is of a maturity to know his roots. Some of the early work by each reflects an indecision, the presence of various possible choices, the hint of a diversity of directions. The reader will find as he follows the selections (which represent of course only a fragment of the total work) that each poet becomes increasingly clear in his rhythms, distinctive in his voice and assured in his thematic explorations. He sloughs various false skins in his progress towards maturity. Donald Davie's tap-root remains in the English eighteenth century; C. H. Sisson's in the English seventeenth century; Thom Gunn's, even – I believe – in his recent free-verse poems, in the sixteenth century; Ted Hughes's energy is identifiably Shakespearian and Jacobean: it is a romanticism from the same source as Wordsworth's, and yet it is not fed from the nineteenth century. There is, of course, a wider diversity of affinities than these, English and foreign, yet to move forward each of these poets has a point of departure particularly his own. This does not imply imitation or discipleship to elder or other poets, rather the tribute which imaginative insight pays: a way of learning through experiencing on the pulse the work of the past and progressing by transposition, analogy and translation. To relate to the tradition in this way is to become a part of it – perhaps a custodian (as any sensitive reader is) and a revivifier, who extends and alters the tradition even as he does so. The reader of Charles Tomlinson's 'The Picture of J. T. in a Prospect of Stone' will return to Marvell's, Coleridge's, Yeats's and Edward Thomas's poems addressed to children with an enriched sense of the generic tradition to which these poems belong. This is a large part of the pleasure the poem affords, over and above the particular and effortlessly symbolic nature of the images rendered. The same can be said of many of the poems here. They enhance and are enhanced by the tradition: their power is not in a relevant but rootless apprehension of the present, but in a rooted apprehension, those roots lying deep in the language and the literature.

The literary history of the post-war years is usually chronicled in terms of 'schools'. Such is the hunger of academics and journalists alike for new material that they are painfully eager to reduce contemporary poetry to the status of 'text' almost before the ink is dry. After the 'Apocalyptics' (with whom Graham's early work was sometimes associated) came 'The Movement' (with which Davie, Gunn, Jennings and Larkin were associated); then came a reaction, and 'The Group' (with which Hughes was very briefly associated). In the 1960s groupings tended to be more regional in bias (Liverpool, Newcastle, Ulster) until, in the 1970s, 'schools' seemed to have taken a recess. Such chronicles of groupings and movements are normally a record of moments of apprenticeship which it suits the categorizing journalist to perpetuate long after the groupings have lost any relevance. The pigeon-holing of poets can hinder our assessment of their work, even if grouping and a group identity assisted in the launching of new talents. Gunn rather resents being associated with The Movement; Elizabeth Jennings never properly belonged to it since its hallmark was a self-deflating irony and she is in no sense an ironist. Critics and journalists, eager for order in the chaos of contemporary writing, become painfully conservative. Not only do they cling to their early, handy categorizations: they resent change in a poet's work, so that, for example, the later poems of R. S. Thomas, Elizabeth Jennings, Ted Hughes and Donald Davie are sometimes taken as an affront. The poet endures from book to book (if he develops) the accusation that he has unfortunately 'fallen off', where in fact he is moving on, avoiding – in Sisson's phrase – 'whatever appears with the face of familiarity', refusing to repeat himself, attempting to extend his language along with his experience.

Privileged as I am to take the longer view, I abandon the task of recent 'literary history' to the Xenophons of journalism and ask the reader to attend not to the action and reaction of one generation and another but to the work of poets who emerged from such apprenticeships (if they went through them) into individual maturity. They emerged thanks to a deeper human sympathy and a more complex and complete knowledge of their art than was possessed by those of their contemporaries who have fallen – or will fall – by the wayside.

Defining something so protean as a 'tradition' is often a matter of saying what it is not, in order to leave a space where it undefinably is. I have argued elsewhere that there is more in common – radically in common – between the work of Philip Larkin and that of William Carlos Williams, the American poet and prosodic innovator, than there is between Larkin and Kingsley Amis, a poet with whom, in conventional terms, Larkin shares a great deal. If Larkin and

Williams are in a common tradition, then that tradition must be perceived as radical. It is not a consensus about style or diction, but rather a determined need on the poet's part to take the language of poetry forward into the world he experiences, and the tact to know what language is fully effective in that world.

Such an inclusive tradition binds Marlowe, Dryden, Wordsworth and Eliot; it is a different sort of tradition, more local to a time and place, that binds Dr Johnson and Oliver Goldsmith, in an age when Johnson could contribute lines to his friend's poems and – such were the agreed conventions and the common degree of skill – the seams hardly showed. The longer tradition I have in mind may be characterized in the present time by a centrality of human concern, often a strong sense of specific locality, an historical consciousness, shared themes – affinities rather than surface similarities. I am not making a qualitative distinction between good and bad poets, but between broadly traditional and more narrowly conventional poets. Kingsley Amis has written good poems. Yet they do not add up in the way Larkin's or Graham's do. They are in a sense peripheral to Amis's other work and to English poetry, while Larkin's are central and, taken together, add up to an important body of work. The less successful poems cannot be written off: they are part of a continuing exploration.

One must avoid, in drawing eleven figures on one canvas, blurring their individual features. It would be hard for the attentive reader to confuse even a line of – for instance – Heaney with a line of Gunn. There is no mistaking the burly Scottish lilt of W. S. Graham for the Welsh acerbity of R. S. Thomas. The humane civilities of Charles Tomlinson have something – but not tone or rhythm – in common with the elegiac opacity of Geoffrey Hill. Ted Hughes's exuberant energy takes him many miles from the sometimes terrifying local clarities of Philip Larkin. The Somerset burr of C. H. Sisson and the still audible Yorkshire of Donald Davie are remote from one another. Accents of place and class, formal choices and dictions, are as different as they can be. The connections lie deeper.

If we look back to Douglas's 'How to Kill' we will see a language heavy with moral overtones consciously deployed in an amoral context. The distance between a language of implicit values, and a world where values are no longer shared, itself becomes a theme for Donald Davie. The function of formal language as an insulator and at the same time a point of contact between isolated individuals is Graham's recurrent theme. The loss of a common civic language (implying as it does the loss of shared faith and shared social objectives) is one of Sisson's themes, while Tomlinson and Hill sometimes explore the gap between the terms of ideology and the events of history those terms seek to interpret and predict, between theory and fact, always with an eye on human consequences. None of the eleven poets is quite free of the strand of religious language and allusion, though each approaches and uses the heritage in a different way. In Graham's poems we will hear echoes of Methodist hymns, hinting at a past in which he belonged to a congregation and a community of believers. For some of the poets here the Christian faith is still true, tested and made more enigmatic and difficult by the history of our time. For others, history has refuted it. Yet none can quite evade it. Hughes struggles strongly with it, inverting it most disturbingly in *Crow*, but it remains a force to be contended with.

Most of these poets share a strong sense of aftermath: the loosening of the historical ties of commonwealth and the translation of systems of values into systems of utility; the exaltation of expediency over truth; the consequent decay in language, institutions, culture and community, and the effect of this decay on the person. The power which reality has over ideas, the unbendable character of the given, has cured British poetry of utopian dreams. The pull of romanticism is still strong, yet it draws the poet who succumbs to it into the dark, not into the light of the imagined millennium.

Such are some of the negative perceptions several of these poets share. A few attempt to derive positive formulations from their experience of faith or vision. Others see it as their function to keep language insistently to its meanings, to teach through a sincere and deliberate accuracy and say no more than they can stand by. They chastise those who, in their view, debase or misuse language, the only possession we still share in common. Others witness to what they see before them: images which they render so carefully and particularly that seeing becomes a form of vision, the fact becomes vividly true in words. Others are caught so deeply in their history that they can write only harsh satire and elegy. Yet none of them is without humour – even if it is a grim humour – and this quality gives proportion to their worlds and is a measure of their self-awareness.

*

The reader of contemporary poetry faces almost as many challenges as the poet does. Given the variety of work, the reader must become a particularist, listening differently from poet to poet. If he can hear Larkin *and* Graham, then I believe he will find much to value in the other nine poets represented here. When he comes to consider the success or otherwise of the poem he might choose to follow Coleridge's example, asking himself what objectives the poet has set himself in the poem, seeing how far the poet has met those objectives, and finally assessing the objectives themselves. Such considerations come *after* the poem has been experienced, not before. Allusions can and should be explored, but only to sharpen the experience of the poem, not to provide it.

Contemporary poetry has suffered from the blackboard and the lecture room. It is a 'subject' which should not need to be taught. It is the writing of our time, and if we have some knowledge of our literature, some feeling for our language and its history, some experience of our society, we should have access to modern poetry without the mediation of exegetes, discussion of 'hidden meanings', puzzlement over the 'relevance' of the message. The sound of the poet's own voice reading, the critical tool-kit and the expert expounder have their place, but it is a secondary one. The good modern poem earns study, but it does not require it.

Sometimes I feel – as a teacher and as a reader – that contemporary poetry aspires to be literature too soon. I am therefore reluctant to offer Johnsonian appraisals of poems which are, for the most part, younger than I am. I recommend them for the pleasure and extension of experience and understanding they provide. 'In our written language', Joubert said, 'there must be voice, soul, space . . . words which exist of themselves and carry their place with them.' Such requisites are met by many of the poems included here. They provide the challenge of diversity. Few of them will be exhausted in a single reading and, in my own experience, a number of them become upon acquaintance valuable additions to the treasure-house of memory, as the good verse of any age will do.

1980   M. SCHMIDT

8

R. S. Thomas

Ronald Stuart Thomas was born in Cardiff in 1913, a year before the
birth of that other Welsh Thomas, Dylan, who so dominated
the stage for better and for worse until, and even after, his death in
1953. In 1953 R. S. Thomas's 'The Minister', a dramatic poem, was
published. Nothing better points up the difference between these
two Welsh writers than a comparison between 'The Minister' and
Under Milk Wood, Dylan Thomas's radio play of about the same
time. In 'The Minister' R. S. Thomas earns the somewhat limited
epithet 'Christian realist'; Dylan Thomas's play has not stood the test
of time so well – his late work being rich in verbal invention and a
kind of cloying sentimentality. While Dylan Thomas has a Welsh
accent, R. S. Thomas has a Welsh voice. His poetry has a civic,
political and – inevitably – a spiritual dimension lacking in Dylan
Thomas's work. In turn, R. S. Thomas lacks the verbal energy and
the psychological dimensions of Dylan Thomas.

Raised in Wales, R. S. Thomas learned the Welsh language as an
adult and studied Welsh poetic forms, some of which affected his
own versification. He was ordained in 1936 as a clergyman of the
Church of Wales. His relations with his largely rural Welsh parishes
and parishioners provided much of his early poetic material. Later
collections have been less particularly rooted in place: a tendency
towards allegory and prophecy and a desire to explore his own
spiritual relations with his God have led to changes that many critics
have lamented. However, the best of the later poems achieve effects
beyond the range of the early Thomas. His early, often traditionally
prosodic poems succeed as it were on the strength of formal com-
petence heightened by a vivid instinct for the apposite but unex-
pected metaphor. The poems are often merely contexts for the
points of vividness, settings for the rare image, but otherwise

9

linguistically dull. In the later poems, the risks taken are more ambitious: the poet gives rein to a formal invention and seeks an overall integration of statement – a greater plainness and a greater depth. It is easier in such a bare style for the poet to fail, and easier for the critic to spot the failures. However, the successes, too, stand out and it is doubtful whether any of the early poems can equal the complete power and candour of some of the later poems, for example 'Pavane' (p. 19).

R. S. Thomas first came to prominence with *Song at the Year's Turning* (1955), a book incorporating earlier collections, with a preface by John Betjeman. Other important collections include *Poetry for Supper* (1958), *Tares* (1964), *The Bread of Truth* (1963), *Pietà* (1966), *Not That He Brought Flowers* (1968), *H'm* (1972), *Laboratories of the Spirit* (1975) and *Frequencies* (1978). His *Selected Poems 1946–1968* appeared in 1973. The development of Thomas's work towards a greater thematic inclusiveness, his changing relation to place, the evolution of his social and spiritual perceptions, and the changes in his forms and his language reveal clearly the growth of an imagination described by John Betjeman as 'not at all literary' – an imagination pursuing what it perceives as 'truth' whatever the consequences for 'beauty'. Thomas's experimentation is never merely play. It is always an earnest engagement with experience and with language.

A Peasant

Iago Prytherch his name, though, be it allowed,
Just an ordinary man of the bald Welsh hills,
Who pens a few sheep in a gap of cloud.
Docking mangels, chipping the green skin
From the yellow bones with a half-witted grin
Of satisfaction, or churning the crude earth
To a stiff sea of clods that glint in the wind –
So are his days spent, his spittled mirth
Rarer than the sun that cracks the cheeks
Of the gaunt sky perhaps once in a week.
And then at night see him fixed in his chair
Motionless, except when he leans to gob in the fire.
There is something frightening in the vacancy of his mind.
His clothes, sour with years of sweat
And animal contact, shock the refined,

But affected, sense with their stark naturalness.
Yet this is your prototype, who, season by season
Against siege of rain and the wind's attrition,
Preserves his stock, an impregnable fortress
Not to be stormed even in death's confusion.
Remember him, then, for he, too, is a winner of wars,
Enduring like a tree under the curious stars.

Song for Gwydion

When I was a child and the soft flesh was forming
Quietly as snow on the bare boughs of bone,
My father brought me trout from the green river
From whose chill lips the water song had flown.

Dull grew their eyes, the beautiful, blithe garland
Of stipples faded, as light shocked the brain;
They were the first sweet sacrifice I tasted,
A young god, ignorant of the blood's stain.

Welsh Landscape

To live in Wales is to be conscious
At dusk of the spilled blood
That went to the making of the wild sky,
Dyeing the immaculate rivers
In all their courses.
It is to be aware,
Above the noisy tractor
And hum of the machine
Of strife in the strung woods,
Vibrant with sped arrows.
You cannot live in the present,
At least not in Wales.
There is the language for instance,
The soft consonants
Strange to the ear.
There are cries in the dark at night
As owls answer the moon,

And thick ambush of shadows,
Hushed at the fields' corners
There is no present in Wales,
And no future;
There is only the past,
Brittle with relics,
Wind-bitten towers and castles
With sham ghosts;
Mouldering quarries and mines;
And an impotent people,
Sick with inbreeding,
Worrying the carcase of an old song.

The Village

Scarcely a street, too few houses
To merit the title; just a way between
The one tavern and the one shop
That leads nowhere and fails at the top
Of the short hill, eaten away
By long erosion of the green tide
Of grass creeping perpetually nearer
This last outpost of time past.

So little happens; the black dog
Cracking his fleas in the hot sun
Is history. Yet the girl who crosses
From door to door moves to a scale
Beyond the bland day's two dimensions.

Stay, then, village, for round you spins
On slow axis a world as vast
And meaningful as any poised
By great Plato's solitary mind.

Taliesin 1952

I have been all men known to history,
Wondering at the world and at time passing;
I have seen evil, and the light blessing
Innocent love under a spring sky.

I have been Merlin wandering in the woods
Of a far country, where the winds waken
Unnatural voices, my mind broken
By sudden acquaintance with man's rage.

I have been Glyn Dŵr set in the vast night,
Scanning the stars for the propitious omen,
A leader of men, yet cursed by the crazed women
Mourning their dead under the same stars.

I have been Goronwy, forced from my own land
To taste the bitterness of the salt ocean;
I have known exile and a wild passion
Of longing changing to a cold ache.

King, beggar and fool, I have been all by turns,
Knowing the body's sweetness, the mind's treason;
Taliesin still, I show you a new world, risen,
Stubborn with beauty, out of the heart's need.

In a Country Church

To one kneeling down no word came,
Only the wind's song, saddening the lips
Of the grave saints, rigid in glass;
Or the dry whisper of unseen wings,
Bats not angels, in the high roof.

Was he balked by silence? He kneeled long,
And saw love in a dark crown
Of thorns blazing, and a winter tree
Golden with fruit of a man's body.

The Return

Coming home was to that:
The white house in the cool grass
Membraned with shadow, the bright stretch
Of stream that was its looking-glass;

And smoke growing above the roof
To a tall tree among whose boughs
The first stars renewed their theme
Of time and death and a man's vows.

Bread

Hunger was loneliness, betrayed
By the pitiless candour of the stars'
Talk, in an old byre he prayed

Not for food; to pray was to know
Waking from a dark dream to find
The white loaf on the white snow;

Not for warmth, warmth brought the rain's
Blurring of the essential point
Of ice probing his raw pain.

He prayed for love, love that would share
His rags' secret; rising he broke
Like sun crumbling the gold air

The live bread for the starved folk.

Genealogy

I was the dweller in the long cave
Of darkness, lining it with the forms
Of bulls. My hand matured early,

But turned to violence: I was the man
Watching later at the grim ford,
Armed with resentment; the quick stream

Remembers at sunset the raw crime.
The deed pursued me; I was the king
At the church keyhole, who saw death

Loping towards me. From that same hour
I fought for right, with the proud chiefs
Setting my name to the broad treaties.

I marched to Bosworth with the Welsh lords
To victory, but regretted after
The white house at the wood's heart.

I was the stranger in the new town,
Whose purse of tears was soon spent;
I filled it with a solider coin

At the dark sources. I stand now
In the hard light of the brief day
Without roots, but with many branches.

Here

I am a man now.
Pass your hand over my brow,
You can feel the place where the brains grow.

I am like a tree,
From my top boughs I can see
The footprints that led up to me.

There is blood in my veins
That has run clear of the stain
Contracted in so many loins.

Why, then, are my hands red
With the blood of so many dead?
Is this where I was misled?

Why are my hands this way
That they will not do as I say?
Does no God hear when I pray?

I have nowhere to go.
The swift satellites show
The clock of my whole being is slow.

It is too late to start
For destinations not of the heart.
I must stay here with my hurt.

The Moor

It was like a church to me.
I entered it on soft foot,
Breath held like a cap in the hand.
It was quiet.
What God was there made himself felt,
Not listened to, in clean colours
That brought a moistening of the eye,
In movement of the wind over grass.

There were no prayers said. But stillness
Of the heart's passions – that was praise
Enough; and the mind's cession
Of its kingdom. I walked on,
Simple and poor, while the air crumbled
And broke on me generously as bread.

The Belfry

I have seen it standing up grey,
Gaunt, as though no sunlight
Could ever thaw out the music
Of its great bell; terrible
In its own way, for religion
Is like that. There are times
When a black frost is upon
One's whole being, and the heart
In its bone belfry hangs and is dumb.

But who is to know? Always,
Even in winter in the cold
Of a stone church, on his knees
Someone is praying, whose prayers fall
Steadily through the hard spell

Of weather that is between God
And himself. Perhaps they are warm rain
That brings the sun and afterwards flowers
On the raw graves and throbbing of bells.

In Church

Often I try
To analyse the quality
Of its silences. Is this where God hides
From my searching? I have stopped to listen,
After the few people have gone,
To the air recomposing itself
For vigil. It has waited like this
Since the stones grouped themselves about it.
These are the hard ribs
Of a body that our prayers have failed
To animate. Shadows advance
From their corners to take possession
Of places the light held
For an hour. The bats resume
Their business. The uneasiness of the pews
Ceases. There is no other sound
In the darkness but the sound of a man
Breathing, testing his faith
On emptiness, nailing his questions
One by one to an untenanted cross.

Concession

Not that he brought flowers
Except for the eyes' blue,
Perishable ones, or that his hands,
Famed for kindness were put then
To such usage; but rather that, going
Through flowers later, she yet could feel
These he spared perhaps for my sake.

Tenancies

This is pain's landscape.
A savage agriculture is practised
Here; every farm has its
Grandfather or grandmother, gnarled hands
On the cheque-book, a long, slow
Pull on the placenta about the neck.
Old lips monopolise the talk
When a friend calls. The children listen
From the kitchen; the children march
With angry patience against the dawn.
They are waiting for someone to die
Whose name is as bitter as the soil
They handle. In clear pools
In the furrows they watch themselves grow old
To the terrible accompaniment of the song
Of the blackbird, that promises them love.

Petition

And I standing in the shade
Have seen it a thousand times
Happen: first theft, then murder;
Rape; the rueful acts
Of the blind hand. I have said
New prayers, or said the old
In a new way. Seeking the poem
In the pain, I have learned
Silence is best, paying for it
With my conscience. I am eyes
Merely, witnessing virtue's
Defeat; seeing the young born
Fair, knowing the cancer
Awaits them. One thing I have asked
Of the disposer of the issues
Of life: that truth should defer
To beauty. It was not granted.

Period

It was a time when wise men
Were not silent, but stifled
By vast noise. They took refuge
In books that were not read.

Two counsellors had the ear
Of the public. One cried 'Buy'
Day and night, and the other,
More plausibly, 'Sell your repose'.

Pavane

Convergences
Of the spirit! What
Century, love? I,
Too; you remember –
Brescia? This sunlight reminds
Of the brocade. I dined
Long. And now the music
Of darkness in your eyes
Sounds. But Brescia,
And the spreading foliage
Of smoke! With Yeats' birds
Grown hoarse.
                    Artificer
Of the years, is this
Your answer? The long dream
Unwound; we followed
Through time to the tryst
With ourselves. But wheels roll
Between and the shadow
Of the plane falls. The
Victim remains
Nameless on the tall
Steps. Master, I
Do not wish, I do not wish
To continue.

Making

And having built it
I set about furnishing it
To my taste: first moss, then grass
Annually renewed, and animals
To divert me: faces stared in
From the wild. I thought up the flowers
Then birds. I found the bacteria
Sheltering in primordial
Darkness and called them forth
To the light. Quickly the earth
Teemed. Yet still an absence
Disturbed me. I slept and dreamed
Of a likeness, fashioning it,
When I woke, to a slow
Music; in love with it
For itself, giving it freedom
To love me; risking the disappointment.

Emerging

Not as in the old days I pray,
God. My life is not what it was.
Yours, too, accepts the presence of
the machine? Once I would have asked
healing. I go now to be doctored,
to drink sinlessly of the blood
of my brother, to lend my flesh
as manuscript of the great poem
of the scalpel. I would have knelt
long, wrestling with you, wearing
you down. Hear my prayer, Lord, hear
my prayer. As though you were deaf, myriads
of mortals have kept up their shrill
cry, explaining your silence by
their unfitness.

It begins to appear
this is not what prayer is about.
It is the annihilation of difference,
the consciousness of myself in you,
of you in me; the emerging
from the adolescence of nature
into the adult geometry
of the mind. I begin to recognize
you anew, God of form and number.
There are questions we are the solution
to, others whose echoes we must expand
to contain. Circular as our way
is, it leads not back to that snake-haunted
garden, but onward to the tall city
of glass that is the laboratory of the spirit.

The Casualty

I had forgotten
    the old quest for truth
        I was here for. Other cares

held me: urgencies
    of the body; a girl
        beckoned; money

had never appeared
    so ethereal; it was God's blood
        circulating in the veins

of creation; I partook
    of it like Communion, lost
        myself on my way

home, with the varying voices
    on call. Moving backward
        into a receding

future, I lost the use
    of perspective, borrowing poetry
        to buy my children

their prose. The past was a poor
            king, rendering his crown down
                  for the historian. Every day

I went on with that
            metallic warfare in which
                  the one casualty is love.

The Calling

And the word came – was it a god
spoke or a devil? – Go
to that lean parish; let them tread
on your dreams; and learn silence

is wisdom. Be alone with yourself
as they are alone in the cold room
of the wind. Listen to the earth
mumbling the monotonous song

of the soil: I am hungry, I
am hungry, in spite of the red dung
of this people. See them go
one by one through that dark door

with the crumpled ticket of your prayers
in their hands. Share their distraught
joy at the dropping of their inane
children. Test your belief

in spirit on their faces staring
at you, on beauty's surrender
to truth, on the soul's selling
of itself for a corner

by the body's fire. Learn the thinness
of the window that is
between you and life, and how
the mind cuts itself if it goes through.

Pilgrimages

There is an island there is no going
to but in a small boat the way
the saints went, travelling the gallery
of the frightened faces of
the long-drowned, munching the gravel
of its beaches. So I have gone
up the salt lane to the building
with the stone altar and the candles
gone out, and kneeled and lifted
my eyes to the furious gargoyle
of the owl that is like a god
gone small and resentful. There
is no body in the stained window
of the sky now. Am I too late?
Were they too late also, those
first pilgrims? He is such a fast
God, always before us and
leaving as we arrive.
                        There are those here
not given to prayer, whose office
is the blank sea that they say daily.
What they listen to is not
hymns but the slow chemistry of the soil
that turns saints' bones to dust,
dust to an irritant of the nostril.

There is no time on this island.
The swinging pendulum of the tide
has no clock; the events
are dateless. These people are not
late or soon; they are just
here with only the one question
to ask, which life answers
by being in them. It is I
who ask. Was the pilgrimage
I made to come to my own
self, to learn that in times
like these and for one like me

God will never be plain and
out there, but dark rather and
inexplicable, as though he were in here?

NOTES

A PEASANT

Iago Prytherch appears, under this and other names, as a type for the Welsh peasant in Thomas's early work.

SONG FOR GWYDION

Gwydion, a figure from Welsh legend, here represents the innocence which is open to the shock of beauty but ignorant of cruelty.

TALIESIN 1952

Taliesin, the legendary British bard, was supposed to have lived in the sixth century. The fourteenth-century *Book of Taliesin* includes work by various hands. The uncertain nature of the bard and the historical and legendary range of work attributed to him make him something of a presiding spirit, a poet who has 'been' magician, king, and victim of oppression, and who understands, as a result, the full scope of human experience.

GENEALOGY

Similar in structure to 'Taliesin 1952', 'Genealogy' is spoken not by a poet but by a figure moving through time from the cave to the council estate, enacting a steady declension from endurance and heroism to a rootless but typical urban existence.

PAVANE

A *pavane* was originally a stately sixteenth-century dance to slow music. Here it implies grave and passionate utterance: the human love of the first half is a richly physical experience in an Italian setting (*Brescia* is in Lombardy, at the foot of the Alps). By contrast, in the second half the speaker returns to his pastoral duties with savage reluctance.

Yeats' birds: see W. B. Yeats, 'Byzantium'.

C. H. Sisson

Charles Hubert Sisson was born in Bristol in 1914. He went to the University of Bristol to read English and later continued his studies in Germany and France. In 1936 he began work in the Civil Service. In 1942 he enlisted and in 1943 was sent on active service to India for a two-and-a-half year tour. In 1945 he returned to England and resumed work in Whitehall. Thirty-six years in the Civil Service took him to Under Secretary and comparable positions in the Ministry of Labour. With his retirement to Somerset, he has continued his literary work, translating Lucretius, Dante and other major texts, and adding to his impressive achievement as an essayist. His poetic work, too, continues.

His generation might be thought to be the one which includes Dylan Thomas, George Barker, David Gascoyne and W. S. Graham. With them, in his later verse, he shares an attitude to the nature of poetic language: the poet's tact is to reject whatever appears 'with the face of familiarity', to express not what he knows already but what he did not know until the poem was written. The essentially involuntary nature of poetic utterance, its *un*-deliberateness, is not a matter of dogma for Sisson, and he has written extended discursive verse; but his best work has its source in other areas, and the notion of a deliberate aesthetic is anathema to him. Unlike other poets of his generation, however, he does not confuse verbal or metaphorical density and obscurity with poetic depth. His language is always lucid and plain. The syntax, however, and the fusion of images, are complex. More than any of his contemporaries, Sisson understands the importance of rhythm as the crucial communicating factor in verse: reason convinces, he quotes a French critic as saying, while rhythm persuades. Some of his poems are metrically regular, but most of them have a dominant and subtle rhythm that owes its expressive freedom to a close reading of the work of Ezra Pound. Sisson is very much in the 'modernist' line; his debts to T. E. Hulme, to Eliot, Ford Madox Ford, Pound, Wyndham Lewis and others he acknowledges. But, like everyone who has learned abiding lessons from these masters, he is not a disciple: a reading of them has freed him from convention and facilitated the development of his distinctive voice. His achievement has been acknowledged by a poet as temperamentally different from him as Donald Davie.

Like R. S. Thomas, Sisson is firmly rooted in a landscape, the landscape of Somerset and the area around Bristol from which he took his early bearings and where he has returned to his retirement. His politics, too, are the particularist politics of English constitutionalism and his religious commitment is to the Church of England, with its political, cultural and spiritual dimensions.

His first important collection of poems, *The London Zoo* (1961) was followed by *Numbers* (1965) and *Metamorphoses* (1968). These books and new work were included in *In The Trojan Ditch: Collected Poems and Selected Translations* (1974). *Anchises* (1976) and *Exactions* (1980) followed. Translations have played an important part in his development, from his early versions of the poems of Heinrich Heine, through his Catullus and Virgil, to Horace, Ovid, Lucretius and Dante. His radical critical volume, *English Poetry 1900–1950* appeared in 1971. Books on Hume, on British administration, on Walter Bagehot, and collections of essays are also an important part of his work. *The Avoidance of Literature,* his collected essays, was published in 1978.

In the Hills

Whereas I wander here among
Stone outcrops, rocks and roots
Below me tapers the peninsula
All India going to the sea.

Below, summer is a disease
Which seas surround whose glassy blue
Nothing can cool and nothing cure
But seize my heart

The jackal wandering in the woods
For I have speech and nothing said
The jackal sniffing in the plains
The vulture and the carrion crow

O jackal, howl about my bed.
O howl around my sleeping head.

The Un-red Deer

The un-red deer
In the un-green forest

The antlers which do not appear
And are not like branches

The hounds which do not bay
With tails which do not swish

The heather beyond and the insignificant stumble
Of the horse not pulled up

By the rider who does not see all this
Nor hear nor smell it

Or does so but it does not matter
The horn sounds Gone away

Or, if it does not, is there hunter,
Hunted, or the broken tree

Swept by the wind from the channel?

Christmas at the Greyhound

'All strangers now; there is nobody that I know.'
Draw near to the hearth; there is one nature of fire.

The Temple

Who are they talking to in the big temple?
If there were a reply it would be a conversation:
It is because there is none that they are fascinated.
What does not reply is the answer to prayer.

Good-Day, Citizen

My life is given over to follies
More than I can exaggerate:
If I told you half you would imagine
That I am a very respectable person.

First, there is the folly of earning money
In order to have what is called independence:
You can admire that quality if you will,
I know what it is and do not admire it.

Secondly, there is the folly of spending it wisely,
So much for insurance, so much for the house,
Suitable provision for the children's education
Which for the most part they would rather not have.

Thirdly there would be, if that were not in fact all,
The supervening graces of domestic virtue
Everything paid up, honest as the day
But I am nearest to my own language in sleep.

A Letter to John Donne

Note: On 27 July, 1617, Donne preached at the parish church at
Sevenoaks, of which he was rector, and was entertained at Knole,
then the country residence of Richard Sackville, third Earl of
Dorset.

I understand you well enough, John Donne
First, that you were a man of ability
Eaten by lust and by the love of God
Then, that you crossed the Sevenoaks High Street
As rector of Saint Nicholas:
I am of that parish.

To be a man of ability is not much
You may see them on the Sevenoaks platform any day
Eager men with despatch cases
Whom ambition drives as they drive the machine
Whom the certainty of meticulous operation
Pleasures as a morbid sex a heart of stone.

That you could have spent your time in the corruption of courts
As these in that of cities, gives you no place among us:
Ability is not even the game of a fool
But the click of a computer operating in a waste
Your cleverness is dismissed from this suit
Bring out your genitals and your theology.

What makes you familiar is this dual obsession;
Lust is not what the rutting stag knows
It is to take Eve's apple and to lose
The stag's paradisal look:
The love of God comes readily
To those who have most need.

You brought body and soul to this church
Walking there through the park alive with deer
But now what animal has climbed into your pulpit?
One whose pretension is that the fear
Of God has heated him into a spirit
An evaporated man no physical ill can hurt.

Well might you hesitate at the Latin gate
Seeing such apes denying the church of God:
I am grateful particularly that you were not a saint
But extravagant whether in bed or in your shroud.
You would understand that in the presence of folly
I am not sanctified but angry.

Come down and speak to the men of ability
On the Sevenoaks platform and tell them
That at your Saint Nicholas the faith
Is not exclusive in the fools it chooses
That the vain, the ambitious and the highly sexed
Are the natural prey of the incarnate Christ.

from *Metamorphoses*

IV

O will you take a fluttering swan
Eurotas, on your plashy banks?

Where the dissimulating bird
Fled from a Venus he had coaxed

Into an eagle with a beak.
Eurotas showed beneath her waves

The rippling image of a girl.
She rose to take the frightened bird

And struggled with him to the bank.
It was the bird came out on top.

Its wings concealed the thing it did
But showed the fluttering legs and hands.

The bird became a stable thing:
There are such dangers for a girl.

Europa felt a sighing bull
Beside her, as she gathered flowers.

It was a gentle, milk-white beast
And tried to graze upon her hair.

She patted and embraced its neck;
Its breath grew deeper as she stroked.

At last she climbed upon his back,
One hand upon a stubby horn.

Over his broad and shaggy cloth
The creature felt the gentle limbs

And in a trice he was away.
Europa held the swimming beast;

She looked at the receding shore
And clutched her garments from the wind.

V

When Virgo crosses with the Ram
Expect a rain of falling stars,

A spilling cornucopia
Betokening plenty, but no peace,

A Danae in her open boat.
The eleemosynary shower

That fell, can now get up again
And it is Easter in the world.

The first age was the age of gold;
The age of iron is our own.

Homo Sapiens
is of No Importance

And it may be that we have no nature
That he could have taken upon him.
Plato of course discussed it.
Deborah sitting under a tree
In a time of matriarchy:
Blessed be thou among women,
Blessed be the hand, the hammer,
Blessed the tent-peg as it drove through Sisera,
Blessed the connection between two interiors,
Blessed the wire between the switch and the bulb.
Not for the mind of Jael but for her hand
Not for the hand but for the hammer
Not for the hammer but for the tent-peg
Not for the peg but for Sisera dead

Not for Sisera dead but for his army routed
Not for that but the momentary ease under a tree
Not for that but for the tree itself
Not for the tree but the sand blowing by it.
If there was any nature it was in that.

The Recollection

In darkness I set out,
  O solstice of my year!
Mindful, though I had none,
  Of crowding ancestors.
And yet I grew in fear
  Although in love also.
The dogs yelped in the street;
  I would not run from them.
Terror and love held still
  The balance where I stood.
Terror pulled down the sky
  But love inclined my feet.
My seedling year grew great
  But did not touch its spring
Unless beside the brooks
  I followed to their source
Or under sprouting ferns
  Or the pale cowslip-cups.
My mind had spread until
  It covered up the sky;
No art could make it wince
  Though sleep would hold it fast.
How long this wakeful dream
  Engulfed me, who can say?
The busy heart beat on
  Until I heard it knock
And then my flesh spoke out:
  'Break through the silken sheet
That hangs before the world
  And bellies in the wind.'
Not I, not I for fear
  Or was it also love?

Or recollection of
   A world more beautiful?
And yet at last a rent
   Came in that silken veil
And, neither in nor out,
   I struggled for my life.
Where has my life passed since?
   In tatters, thorns and shreds,
Under the briar I creep;
   The puddle is my drink.
The pebbles in the path
   Are my extremest stars.
Who treads that Milky Way?
   Some giant, but not I.
I am the broken chalk
   Under his foot, the twig
That lies across his path.
   High summer came and went;
I did not find my God
   Although my body bore
The impress of a cross,
   Faint, almost negligible.
And now the autumn comes
   With pounding strides, and day
Closes her weary eye,
   I find no trace of peace
Nor vigour for the war
   And God looks down upon
One who does not look up.
   The heavens, which held my mind,
Have closed, and left me small.
   Saint Thomas now brings in
My last and shortest day.
   I seek my terminal.
The candle gutters fast.
   Along the corridor
The last footfall is lost.
   There is no friend but God;
On him I may presume
   Because He does not come.
O could I have that mind
   I carried in the womb,
Which knew, but could not say,
   This solstice would be birth.

The Person

What is the person? Is it hope?
If so, there is no I in me.
    Is it a trope
Or paraphrase of deity?
    If so,
I may be what I do not know.

Do not be proud of consciousness
For happiness is in the skin.
    What you possess
Is what another travels in.
    Your light
Is phosphorus in another's night.

It does not matter what you say
For any what or who you are
    Is of a day
Which quite extinguishes your star –
    Not speech
But what your feelers cannot reach.

There is one God we do not know
Stretched on Orion for a cross
    And we below
In several sorts of lesser loss
    Are we
In number not identity.

Evening

Sleep has my muscles and a cord my throat.
Faint heart! The rooks at evening repair,
Climbing upon so many steps on air,
To the elm tops: caw, on the balustrade,
Caw from the church-tower, where the dead are laid
Under a passing shadow. I to tea,
Beside the fire in the old house, quietly.

The Usk

Christ is the language which we speak to God
And also God, so that we speak in truth;
He in us, we in him, speaking
To one another, to him, the City of God.

I

Such a fool as I am you had better ignore
Tongue twist, malevolent, fat mouthed
I have no language but that other one
His the Devil's, no mouse I, creeping out of the cheese
With a peaked cap scanning the distance
Looking for truth.
Words when I have them, come out, the Devil
Encouraging, grinning from the other side of the street
And my tears
Streaming, a blubbered face, when I am not laughing
Where in all this
Is calm, measure,
Exactness
The Lord's peace?

II

Nothing is in my own voice because I have not
Any. Nothing in my own name
Here inscribed on water, nothing but flow
A ripple, outwards. Standing beside the Usk
You flow like truth, river, I will get in
Over me, through me perhaps, river let me be crystalline
As I shall not be, shivering upon the bank.
A swan passed. So is it, the surface, sometimes
Benign like a mirror, but not I passing, the bird.

III

Under the bridge, meet reward, the water
Falling in cascades or worse, you devil, for truthfulness
Is no part of the illusion, the clear sky

35

Is not yours, the water
Falling not yours
Only the sheep
Munching at the river brim
Perhaps

IV

What I had hoped for, the clear line
Tremulous like water but
Clear also to the stones underneath
Has not come that way, for my truth
Was not public enough, nor perhaps true.
Holy Father, Almighty God
Stop me before I speak

– per Christum.

V

Lies on my tongue. Get up and bolt the door
For I am coming not to be believed
The messenger of anything I say.
So I am come, stand in the cold to tonight
The servant of the grain upon my tongue,
Beware, I am the man, and let me in.

VI

So speech is treasured, for the things it gives
Which I can not have, for I speak too plain
Yet not so plain as to be understood
It is confusion and a madman's tongue.
Where drops the reason, there is no one by.
Torture my mind: and so swim through the night
As envy cannot touch you, or myself
Sleep comes, and let her, warm at my side, like death.
The Holy Spirit and the Holy One
Of Israel be my guide. So among tombs
Truth may be sought, and found, if we rejoice
With Ham and Shem and Japhet in the dark
The ark rolls onward over a wide sea.
Come sleep, come lightning, comes the dove at last.

Sumptuary Laws

Still with the hope of being understood,
Of understanding myself
Or understanding someone else,
I engaged in restless action.
It was no good.
First because
It had no issue, secondly because
If it could have had, I would no longer care.
The problems of age are semblant, one thing
Like another, no thing identical,
The things having been seen, the passions
Expended in better times by a better man.
So outwardly and above
We turn, gracious and empty
The old hypocrites, counting the stars,
Loving the children, counting them like money.
Thanking what stars we have that the wrong turnings
Have all been taken, a life of comfort
Assured, as it may be, to the last deception
I could call this life respectable but
I must call it mine, which is worse.

In Spring-Time

Another time, this way the primrose,
I lost my way before my age was full
In a deep valley. And the cleft said nothing
But perhaps, I am limestone, grey
Lichen upon me, grey.

No voice. Came summer yet no voice. Came once
The lark, the plover and the hare in March.
Almost the wind is speech.

What turns I took and then the cock-crow came
Not once but many times.

Gardening

What night, corrupt, as this must be, with dreams
Gathers around this age that finds me now
Here in this garden, not in Eden, no
Another garden and another time

But there is neither slope nor sun can make
Amends for what I missed under your hands.
Old fool. Reproaches I could buy for nothing
In any market-place. How can I turn
This ageing sorrow to a biting wind
To catch me like the tangles of your hair
Gone and imagined? Better than dreams
Is closing in the circle of the earth
Time out of mind.

Marcus Aurelius

I do not want to pour out my heart any more
Like a nightingale bursting or a tap dripping:
Father no more verses on me, Marcus Aurelius
I will be an emperor and think like you.

Quiet, dignified, stretched out under a clothes line
The garden of my soul is open for inspection
As the gardener left it, chaque cheveu à sa place
And if you do not believe me you can comb through my
                                        papers yourself.

Of course you may not agree with: No hurt because the lips
                                        are tight.
The psychologists have been too much for you, but that
                                        rascal Freud
Did nothing but devise his own superficial entanglements
For his readers to trip over, while he smiled.

Old devil of Vienna, moving among the porcelain,
You were the beetle under the ruins of an empire
And where the Habsburgs had protruded their lips
You pinched your nostrils.

If I were a plain man I would do the same,
Dexterous, money-making, conforming to another pattern
Than the one I seek which will cover me entirely:
I hope to be an emperor under my own mausoleum.

Over the Wall

Berlin, May 1975

I

He will go over and tell the king
Or whoever is top dog in that country
How there is feasting here, the wastes are empty
The nine governors sleeping

Not a prophetic sleep, with the lids opening
Upon passion, dreaming of conflict
But the eyes turned inwards so that the whites
Gaze upon the world, and the heart ticks steadily
To the combustion of a strange engine
Not in the heart, more like a bee
Buzzing in the neighbourhood. Lost heart, lost head
There is no reflection under the cool brain
Which thinks only of last night's dominoes,
Glibly at least. Over the wall,
Knives drawn, teeth drawn back,
Swallowing the rattle they make in case the night
Should interpret their wishes.
Here in the west, far west, slumber
While death collects his paces.

I am not warlike but, once the frontiers are falling
Each man must put on his belt, it has been done before
And the whimpering must stop, Death being the kingdom
Of this world.

2

I have seen the doomed city, it was not my own
Love has no city like this, with barred hatreds
All bitterness, all shames. I do not think there is any
Feast to be eaten or long shawls
Trailed in the dust before the fanatic mob
Only quiet people live here, eating their sandwiches
Under the lilac while the boats go by,
Interminable imitation of reality
Which is not to be had, and should the frost fall
Should the eagle turn its head
The city of too many desperate adventures
I have seen them all, or so it seems, the Uhlans . . .
And now from the steppes
It is as if the Sarmatian horsemen came back,
Yet they do not stir, or make themselves visible . . .
One street I remember
There is no majesty in its lost endeavours
Speak to me no more, I have heard only
The marching men.
Sleep comes to those who deserve
Funerals under the chipped archways.

3

I do not think this is the end of the story
There are battalions enough behind the wall.
The tall policemen bent over me like the priest
Of an evil religion, as if I were the elements
And he the emissary who was empowered to transform me.
That was not the same
Dream-ridden solitude I had known before
Where a flame climbed the walls there was no one by.

4

I know only aspen, beech, oak
But here on these wastes the turtle
Sang among the sands, sitting upon a pine-tree
No man has meditated this regress
Yet the afternoon sun falls upon faces
Less tame than tigers.

Swimming the Horses

To Pippa and David Wright

Swimming the horses at Appleby in Westmorland
– Or Cumbria as they now call it, God damn their eyes.
The rest of the verses *desunt*: they were meant to say
Damn all politicians and bureaucrats
Who cannot make fires with uncertain materials.
They imagine that their voices will be heard above
The ripple of rivers and the song of cuckoos –
Which they will not be, or not for long
If they continue with their inordinate charges
To feed reputatious mouths, or none at all
And think that generations of mud-eaters
Can be stamped out to serve a committee slicker
– As they can indeed, but eaten by a dust
That will soon settle over the whole of England.
Those who kick their ancestors in the teeth
Prosper for a time, but in adversity,
Which soon comes, there is a change.

Est in Conspectu Tenedos

I

The day goes slowly, it is the first day
After the fall of Troy. I walk upon the beaches,
A ghost among ghosts, but the most shadowy I
O Tenedos O the thin island
Hiding the ships. They need not hide from me
I am the least figure upon the shore,
Which the wind does not notice, the water refract, or the
                                              sands count
As one of their number. I was a warrior,
Yes, in Troy
Before all reason was lost.

Where did Helen come from? Where is she now?
All reason is lost and so is she.
I was only a parcel of her reason
Now of her loss
Ghosts
Cannot be companionable; parts, shreds,
All that I am, ghost of a part of a part

2

Desolate shore, dark night
I have lost so much that I am not now myself
That lost it, I am the broken wind
The lost eagle flying, the dawn
Rising over Tenedos

3

Not any more I, that is the last thing
Rise or fall, sunrise or sunset
It is all one. The moon is not friendly
No, nor the sun
Nor darkness, nor
Even the bands of maidens bringing offerings
Pouring libations, buried
Among the ineluctable dead.

4

Dead, ineluctable, certain
The fate of all men.

Narcissus

corpus putat esse, quod umbra est

If I could only find a little stream
Which leapt out of the ground over black pebbles
And wore a hat of light on every ripple,
I should not care for the imaginary
Problems of I and Me, or Who or Why.

C. H. SISSON

This corner of the world would be my mind;
What it saw I would say, if it were cloud,
Blue sky or even wind told by an eddy:
But what I would not see is this body,
Aged, severe and, written on it, REFUSE.
If that came back into my little stream
It might be I should wake shrieking from my dream.
To what? Ah, what is there for us to wake to?
When pain is past, that is our hope or pleasure.
But nail that nothing now, keep me in vain
Beside the water, not seeing any shadow,
Only translucence, only the pebbles and earth,
A weed swaying, a fish, but nothing human
Or bearing any resemblance to man or woman.
Nothing compels our nature to this shape
For a stone will resemble the friends we make.
The mind is not peculiarly under skin
But might lie loose upon a high mountain.
A corner of a cloud would do for a mind,
The bright border perhaps, with the moon behind,
The wind, recognized by its wandering billow
Scattering to surf as the moon comes and goes.
I thought I was a man because I was taught so.

Moon-Rise

It is the evening brought me here,
Or I the evening.
So I, which is the writing finger,
The hand placed on the sill, the night
Coming up from beyond Kingsbury:

Another foot, or hand, perhaps,
Perhaps a train, passing along
Down the line by the signal box;
Or that rising star which may be
The next to come out of the west.
Which way? has no meaning, because
Here and there relate to what:
The moon rises, as we say.

Nightingale, you sing no more;
The tree you sat on is not there;
The night you sang has also gone:
And I alone remember you,
Or am the nightingale tonight.

Night of the day, because succeeding;
Or of the night, because pleading;
Or of the Lamb of God because
Bleeding.
Useless to ask any question of
This night or any:
Answer as lightly as you ask.

The Red Admiral

The wings tremble, it is the red admiral
Ecstatically against the garden wall;
September is his enjoyment, but he does not know it,
Name it, or refer to it at all.

The old light fades upon the old stones;
The day is old: how is there such light
From grey clouds? It is the autumnal equinox
And we shall all have shrunk before daylight.

A woman, a horse and a walnut-tree: old voices
Out of recessed time, in the cracks,
It may be, where the plaster has crumbled:
But the butterfly hugs the blue lias.

The mystery is only the close of day,
Remembered love, which is also present:
Layer upon layer, old times, the fish turning
Once more in the pond, and the absent.

All could not be at once without memory
Crowding out what cannot be remembered;
Better to have none, best of all when
The evening sunlight has ended.

Its fingers lighter than spiders, the red admiral
Considers, as I do, with little movement;
With little of anything that is meant:
But let the meaning go, movement is all.

Autumn Poems

I

En rond, nous sommes en rond
Ainsi, nous danserons

The plunging year, the bright year. Through the clouds
Comes sunlight, sunlight, making iron-grey
The under-belly of the cloud it comes from.
Golden the dull leaves September wants to turn,
But dust is everywhere, not free, but plastered
Thinly over road, pavements, even bark
Branches and leaves, and the old iron buildings,
Ochre walls, fall. Not so, and yet it seems so.
Dust is the country way and dust the rhyme
Which equals everything in this sad time.

2

Broken-backed willow, elder and the sharp tree
Which is loaded with berries presently,
Heap upon heap, hawthorn, while the rose-hip
Beside her offers me her paler lip.

3

The world which was not mine, should I have wanted it?
By eating deceived, as Adam was,
I tell myself, but I do not believe it:
Belief is difficult after sixty years.

4

Once there was bitterness which had regret in it
Or even hope, now there is none of these;
The bitterness itself is muted,
Not by satisfaction, which is not
But by etiolation, defoliation, the leaves
Growing whiter and thinner, and no wind through them.

Once I found sleep, it was
In the hollow of anybody else's hand
As the world sleeps in God's; now there is waking:
Not to receive the world, as some do,
But to watch, as the old, suspiciously.

I am looking for contentment out of nothing
For new things are made out of what is new
And I have none except this: the birds' song,
The rain, the evening sky, the grass on the lawn.

5

I am a tree: mark how the leaves grow
Sparsely now; here a bunch, there,
At the end of this thin twig, another
And the bark hardening, thickening. I am allowed
No respite from the wind, the long
Thorn trunk and branches stretching like a swan's neck
In torment. And the hiss
My own malice makes of this wind
Gentle enough, in itself: I can imagine myself
As this tree but what consciousness
Should go with it – that,
Screeching neck, I am blind to.

In Flood

A word for everybody, myself nobody,
Hardly a ripple over the wide mere:
There is the winter sunshine over the water,
The spirits everywhere, myself here.

Do you know it? It is Arthur's territory
– Agravaine, Mordred, Guinevere and Igraine –
Do you hear them? Or see them in the distant sparkle?
Likely not, but they are there all the same.

And I who am here, actually and statistically,
Have a wide absence as I look at the sea,
Waters which 'wap and wan', Malory said –
And the battle-pile of those he accounted dead.

Yet his word breathes still upon the ripple
Which is innumerable but, more like a leaf
Curled in autumn and blown through the winter,
I on this hill-side take my last of life:

Only glad that when I go to join them
I shall be speechless, no-one will ask my name,
Yet among the named dead I shall be gathered,
Speaking to no man, not spoken of, but in place.

NOTES

IN THE HILLS

During the Second World War, Sisson was on active service in India
and on the North West Frontier, as a British soldier.

A LETTER TO JOHN DONNE

the Latin gate: a reference to Donne's attraction to Roman Catholic-
ism, before he took Anglican orders.

from METAMORPHOSES

These sections form part of a longer poem, which is loosely based on
Ovid's great Latin poem of the same title. It narrates a series of
classical myths that centre on the theme of transformation. In his
poem Sisson interleaves classical and biblical stories. He unites the
two radical traditions of European culture in the Incarnation, a
process of imaginative integration his poetry often effects:

> The metamorphosis of all.
> Or he was nothing but a child . . .

There is a qualifying irony throughout the poem, a refusal to assert a
truth of which he was not at the time certain.

Eurotas: a river in the south of the Peloponnese.

Europa: daughter of the King of Tyre, abducted by Zeus in the
form of a bull.

When Virgo crosses with the Ram: an astrological conjunction.

Danae: daughter of the King of Argos, visited by Zeus in a golden
shower, gave birth to Perseus.

eleemosynary shower: the rain of gold, the form Zeus took
('eleemosynary' has to do with alms and alms-giving; the word
provides a crucial semantic bridge to the biblical theme).

HOMO SAPIENS IS OF NO IMPORTANCE

Deborah, a Hebrew prophetess and judge, decided disputes beneath a tree known as 'Deborah's palm'. When Jabin, King of Canaan, oppressed Israel, she and Barak organized his defeat (see Judges 5–6). *Sisera*, commander of Jabin's army, was murdered by *Jael* in Deborah's tent. She drove a tent-peg through his temple as he lay sleeping. The poem pursues a central theme of Sisson's: what is the specific, definable and perceptible nature of man? As the culture which provides a context for the development of the person decays or is destroyed, roots and continuities are lost, perspectives become foreshortened, the question becomes harder to ask and to answer.

THE RECOLLECTION

St Thomas the Apostle is celebrated on 21 December, the winter solstice. The poem, progressing through the year and through a life, comes to rest on intellectual and spiritual doubt – like Thomas's – and a residual belief the speaker wishes to revitalize on the eve of Christmas.

THE USK

The River Usk, in Wales, is closely associated with Henry Vaughan (1621?–95), the metaphysical poet who owed a profound debt to the greatest Anglican poet, George Herbert. Vaughan styled himself 'Olor Iscanus' ('Swan of Usk'). He frequently exploits the symbol of water as baptism and absolution in his poetry. Sisson, indebted to Vaughan and his landscape, develops tentatively in this poem the theme of absolution. The episodes of Genesis 6–10 provide further material for Sisson, who also echoes the New Testament and the Anglican liturgy. Despite its literary and theological affinities, 'The Usk' is anything but a 'literary' poem: its idiom is very much Sisson's own, and the experience it enacts, too, is real. Vaughan is part of his Anglicanism and part of his natural world. (See Sisson's essay, 'Songs in the Night: The Work of Henry Vaughan the Silurist', in *The Avoidance of Literature* (1978). The essay was written at much the same time as the poem.)

Ham and Shem and Japhet: sons of Noah who, with him, built the Ark and survived the Flood.

SUMPTUARY LAWS

These are laws which regulate expenditure to restrain excess.

IN SPRING-TIME

The closing lines cannot but recall Good Friday (Matthew 26: 69–75).

MARCUS AURELIUS

This was the second-century Roman emperor and stoic philosopher whose *Meditations* were written in Greek in twelve books. At his accession a new age was expected – an age such as Plato had foreseen under a philosopher king. Instead, the reign was marked by unprecedented defeats and disasters. Yet the emperor's great book survives.

Old devil of Vienna: Freud.

Habsburgs: the royal Austrian family who contrast with Marcus Aurelius's more severe, and Freud's more fastidious, style.

OVER THE WALL

This reference is to the Berlin Wall. Sisson lived as a student in Berlin before the Second World War. This poem, written on a return visit in 1975, conflates the experiences of then and now, finding the surface altered but an underlying continuity – a terrifying continuity which goes deep in history.

Uhlans: a type of cavalryman or lancer.

Sarmatian: a warlike peoples from the area now occupied (roughly speaking) by Russia and Poland.

SWIMMING THE HORSES

The poem begins to describe the annual gipsy gathering in Appleby in Westmorland. The poet's reflections are interrupted by the recollection that a trivial bureaucratic manoeuvre has abolished Westmorland, creating a new county called Cumbria, without historic or cultural sanction. This casual rejection of continuities will have serious consequences. It is typical of other forms of mindless change.

EST IN CONSPECTU TENEDOS

The title is from Virgil's *Aeneid* II, 21 –

> Est in conspectu Tenedos, notissima fama
> insula . . .

– the beginning of Aeneas's narration of the final stage of the Trojan war, when the Greek ships withdrew behind the island of Tenedos, leaving behind the wooden horse with its cargo of warriors. The Earl of Surrey (1517–47) translated the relevant passage as follows:

> There stands in sight an isle hight Tenedon,
> Rich and of fame while Priam's city stood:
> Now but a bay, and road unsure for ship.
> Hither them secretly the Greeks withdrew,
> Shrouding themselves under the desert shore.
> And, weening we they had been fled and gone,
> And with the winds had fet the land of Greece,
> Troye discharged her long continued dole.
> The gates cast up, we issued out to play,
> The Greekish camp desirous to behold,
> The places void and the forsaken coasts.

ineluctable: unable to be avoided or escaped from. Dead and living are similarly snared and cannot struggle free.

NARCISSUS

The epigraph, from Ovid's *Metamorphoses* (book III): 'He takes for substance what is merely shade'. The conventional, self-regarding figure of Narcissus is here transformed into a figure who regards the absence of self.

AUTUMN POEMS

Sisson bases his epigraph on Old French troubadour poetry: 'Round and round, we dance in a round, thus we shall dance'.

IN FLOOD

Arthur's territory: the West Country, especially Sisson's own shire, Somerset, the landscape that informs many of his poems.

Malory: Sir Thomas Malory (d. 1471), whose prose narrative *Morte d'Arthur* chronicled the legendary deeds of Arthur and his court.

W. S. Graham

William Sydney Graham was born in a tenement in Greenock, Scotland, in 1918. He was brought up on Clydeside, attending Greenock High School and later spending a year at the Workers' Educational Association College near Edinburgh. He was a lecturer at New York University (1947–8). For many years now he has lived in Madron, Cornwall, an area which plays an important role in his poems. He remains a Scot in accent and, to some degree, in orientation: there is a 'Scots timbre' in his poetic voice and the reader can sense how deeply this runs by noting the skill with which Graham can change tone, in a single line, from raucousness to tenderness, from hectoring to a whisper. This skill is characteristic of verse in Scottish dialect: to achieve it in standard English is no mean feat. It depends very much on the presence of a defined voice behind the poems.

In achieving this idiosyncratic and individual voice, Graham has come a long way from his earliest work. He began publishing in the long shadow of Dylan Thomas and the 'apocalyptic' poets, and his early work, rich in verbal inventiveness, suffers from a rhythmic monotony and an uncertainty of theme. The early poems are perplexing in a different way from the later work, where a very plain diction and syntax are animated by strong and expressive rhythms and a surprising variety of modulations of tone. Graham owes debts to Dylan Thomas, to be sure, in his early work. His later work, however, has been affected by the great modernist writers, including T. S. Eliot and Samuel Beckett. He acknowledges these debts, as well as debts to James Joyce, Marianne Moore and Ezra Pound. To this list should be added the name of Gerard Manley Hopkins. Perhaps the discovery of the *dramatic* in the dramatic monologue form has done more to bring his verse to its distinctive excellence than anything else. His development is a gaining of courage to speak as he would speak, disregarding prosodic conventions and finding a voice deep in himself. His theme is, as often as not in his mature work, language, its value in fending off silence, its limited capacity for communication. His relations with the reader are ambivalent – he normally addresses a reader or another person in his poems. He explores the paradoxical nature of poetic statement, which moves in time but, as it were, arrests time. He addresses his own past, the dead, the future, from within the poem, no longer time-bound. This is a privileged vantage-point which carries with it the sense of the limitation of poetic utterance (and of language itself) *within* the world of passing silences. There is the added irony that the *finished* poem excludes the poet, too.

His collections include *Cage Without Grievance* (1942), *2nd Poems* (1945), *The White Threshold* (1949), *The Nightfishing* (1955), *Malcolm Mooney's Land* (1970) and *Implements In Their Places* (1977). The *Collected Poems 1942–1977* appeared in 1979. Graham's first major poem was 'The Nightfishing', unfortunately too long to be included in this collection. In the interests of representing the full range of his work, the excellent long poem 'Malcolm Mooney's Land' was also omitted. Graham has defined his themes, first in negative terms, as 'the difficulty of communication; the difficulty of speaking from a fluid identity'; and then, more positively, as 'the lessons in physical phenomena; the mystery and adequacy of the aesthetic experience; the elation of being alive in the language'.

O Gentle Queen of the Afternoon

O gentle queen of the afternoon
Wave the last orient of tears.
No daylight comet ever breaks
On so sweet an archipelago
As love on love.

The fundamental negress built
In a cloudy descant of the stars
Surveys no sorrow, invents no limits
Till laughter the watcher of accident
Sways off to God.

W. S. GRAHAM

O gentle queen of the afternoon
The dawn is rescued dead and risen.
Promise, O bush of blushing joy,
No daylight comet ever breaks
On so sweet an archipelago
As love on love.

Let Me Measure My Prayer
with Sleep

Let me measure my prayer with sleep as an
Infant of story in the stronghold eyelid
Left by a hedge with a badge of campions
Beats thunder for moles in the cheek of Spring.

Stronghold till squall robs holiday within
This wonder where twin hills back the eyes
Holds weeds and geometry in a girdered hive.

God will hear all that pastoral can tell
Where this throe this offence to where I walk
Propels in hemispheres through rook and rowan.

So to go counter magnify my dress.
Let swimmers tussle fatal as the fools
That all the bones of anarchy can tell.

And inland sleeps the sorrel and silverweed
Not less in gardens where the bliss is heard
Climbing the well of unrecurring cures.

Let me measure my trade with a tented sleep
Where none shall in heart's ease landlord love.
Leave me for child's sake hubbed in harebells
Where planets in pasture magnify my face.

Gigha

That firewood pale with salt and burning green
Outfloats its men who waved with a sound of drowning
Their saltcut hands over mazes of this rough bay.

Quietly this morning beside the subsided herds
Of water I walk. The children wade the shallows.
The sun with long legs wades into the sea.

To My Brother

Alistair approach this thirty
Lines with a homing memory.
Each step speaks out the springtime.
Our Clydeside merges home.

The morning rises up.
The sun's enamoured step
Crosses the ancient firth.
Your breath crosses my breath.

The sun's encouraged step,
The released word's escape,
Enters the bright bright world
Held in the helmet head.

The firth makes light of us
Exchanged on those waters
Between Gareloch and Greenock
Wearing woodshell and rowlock.

All on this emerged morning
Between banks of shipbuilding
The distilled and hurtled out
Industry of mind and heart

Floats us from hammer yards,
Twin measures of these words.
Foreseen secretly by
Violence and strawdeath eye

As the cairns move against
The natural seamist
We sail for ever the authorities
Of a changed firth's waters.

I let thirty lines loose.
These words make light of us.

Listen Put On Morning

Listen. Put on morning.
Waken into falling light.
A man's imagining
Suddenly may inherit
The handclapping centuries
Of his one minute on earth.
And hear the virgin juries
Talk with his own breath
To the corner boys of his street.
And hear the Black Maria
Searching the town at night.
And hear the playropes caa
The sister Mary in.
And hear Willie and Davie
Among bracken of Narnain
Sing in a mist heavy
With myrtle and listeners.
And hear the higher town
Weep a petition of fears
At the poorhouse close upon
The public heartbeat.
And hear the children tig
And run with my own feet
Into the netting drag

Of a suiciding principle.
Listen. Put on lightbreak.
Waken into miracle.
The audience lies awake
Under the tenements
Under the sugar docks
Under the printed moments.
The centuries turn their locks
And open under the hill
Their inherited books and doors
All gathered to distil
Like happy berry pickers
One voice to talk to us.
Yes listen. It carries away
The second and the years
Till the heart's in a jacket of snow
And the head's in a helmet white
And the song sleeps to be wakened
By the morning ear bright.
Listen. Put on morning.
Waken into falling light.

Yours Truly

In reply to your last letter
Which came in too confused
For words saying 'Listen.
And silence even has turned
Away. Listen.' Dear Pen
Pal in the distance, beyond
My means, why do you bring
Your face down so near
To affront me here again
With a new expression out
Of not indifferent eyes?
I know you well alas
From where I sit behind
The Art barrier of ice.

Did you hear me call you across
The dead centre of the night?

Where is your pride I said
To myself calling myself
By my name even pronouncing
It freshly I thought but blushed
At the lonely idea.
I saw myself wearing
A clumping taliped
Disguise I was too shy
To take an answer from.

Am I too loud? I hear
Members of the house stirring
Not able to keep asleep
Not able to keep awake
Nor to be satisfactorily
Between. O by the way
I thought I saw you standing
Older losing yourself in
The changed Mooney's mirrors
Of what is left of Ireland.

The Thermal Stair

For the painter Peter Lanyon
killed in a gliding accident 1964

I called today, Peter, and you were away.
I look out over Botallack and over Ding
Dong and Levant and over the jasper sea.

Find me a thermal to speak and soar to you from
Over Lanyon Quoit and the circling stones standing
High on the moor over Gurnard's Head where some

Time three foxglove summers ago, you came.
The days are shortening over Little Parc Owles.
The poet or painter steers his life to maim

Himself somehow for the job. His job is Love
Imagined into words or paint to make
An object that will stand and will not move.

Peter, I called and you were away, speaking
Only through what you made and at your best.
Look, there above Botallack, the buzzard riding

The salt updraught slides off the broken air
And out of sight to quarter a new place.
The Celtic sea, the Methodist sea is there.

You said once in the Engine
House below Morvah
That words make their world
In the same way as the painter's
Mark surprises him
Into seeing new.
Sit here on the sparstone
In this ruin where
Once the early beam
Engine pounded and broke
The air with industry.

Now the chuck of daws
And the listening sea.

'Shall we go down' you said
'Before the light goes
And stand under the old
Tinworkings around
Morvah and St Just?'
You said 'Here is the sea
Made by alfred wallis
Or any poet or painter's
Eye it encountered.
Or is it better made
By all those vesselled men
Sometime it maintained?
We all make it again.'

Give me your hand, Peter,
To steady me on the word.

Seventy-two by sixty,
Italy hangs on the wall.
A woman stands with a drink
In some polite place

And looks at SARACINESCO
And turns to mention space.
That one if she could
Would ride Artistically
The thermals you once rode.

Peter, the phallic boys
Begin to wink their lights.
Godrevy and the Wolf
Are calling Opening Time.
We'll take the quickest way
The tin singers made.
Climb here where the hand
Will not grasp on air.
And that dark-suited man
Has set the dominoes out
On the Queen's table.
Peter, we'll sit and drink
And go in the sea's roar
To Labrador with wallis
Or rise on Lanyon's stair.

Uneasy, lovable man, give me your painting
Hand to steady me taking the word-road home.
Lanyon, why is it you're earlier away?
Remember me wherever you listen from.
Lanyon, dingdong dingdong from carn to carn.
It seems tonight all Closing bells are tolling
Across the Duchy shire wherever I turn.

Imagine a Forest

Imagine a forest
A real forest.

You are walking in it and it sighs
Round you where you go in a deep
Ballad on the border of a time
You have seemed to walk in before.
It is nightfall and you go through
Trying to find between the twittering

59

Shades the early starlight edge
Of the open moor land you know.
I have set you here and it is not a dream
I put you through. Go on between
The elephant bark of those beeches
Into that lightening, almost glade.

   And he has taken
   My word and gone

Through his own Ettrick darkening
Upon himself and he's come across
A glinted knight lying dying
On needles under a high tree.
Ease his visor open gently
To reveal whatever white, encased
Face will ask out at you who
It is you are or if you will
Finish him off. His eyes are open.
Imagine he does not speak. Only
His beard moving against the metal
Signs that he would like to speak.

   Imagine a room
   Where you are home

Taking your boots off from the wood
In that deep ballad very not
A dream and the fire noisily
Kindling up and breaking its sticks.
Do not imagine I put you there
For nothing. I put you through it
There in that holt of words between
The bearded liveoaks and the beeches
For you to meet a man alone
Slipping out of whatever cause
He thought he lay there dying for.

   Hang up the ballad
   Behind the door.

You are come home but you are about
To not fight hard enough and die
In a no less desolate dark wood
Where a stranger shall never enter.

   Imagine a forest
   A real forest.

Johann Joachim Quantz's
Five Lessons

The First Lesson

So that each person may quickly find that
Which particularly concerns him, certain metaphors
Convenient to us within the compass of this
Lesson are to be allowed. It is best I sit
Here where I am to speak on the other side
Of language. You, of course, in your own time
And incident (I speak in the small hours.)
Will listen from your side. I am very pleased
We have sought us out. No doubt you have read
My Flute Book. Come. The Guild clock's iron men
Are striking out their few deserted hours
And here from my high window Brueghel's winter
Locks the canal below. I blow my fingers.

The Second Lesson

Good morning, Karl. Sit down. I have been thinking
About your progress and my progress as one
Who teaches you, a young man with talent
And the rarer gift of application. I think
You must now be becoming a musician
Of a certain calibre. It is right maybe
That in our lessons now I should expect
Slight and very polite impatiences
To show in you. Karl, I think it is true,
You are now nearly able to play the flute.

Now we must try higher, aware of the terrible
Shapes of silence sitting outside your ear
Anxious to define you and really love you.
Remember silence is curious about its opposite
Element which you shall learn to represent.

Enough of that. Now stand in the correct position
So that the wood of the floor will come up through you.

Stand, but not too stiff. Keep your elbows down.
Now take a simple breath and make me a shape
Of clear unchained started and finished tones.
Karl, as well as you are able, stop
Your fingers into the breathing apertures
And speak and make the cylinder delight us.

The Third Lesson

Karl, you are late. The traverse flute is not
A study to take lightly. I am cold waiting.
Put one piece of coal in the stove. This lesson
Shall not be prolonged. Right. Stand in your place.

Ready? Blow me a little ladder of sound
From a good stance so that you feel the heavy
Press of the floor coming up through you and
Keeping your pitch and tone in character.

Now that is something, Karl. You are getting on.
Unswell your head. One more piece of coal.
Go on now but remember it must be always
Easy and flowing. Light and shadow must
Be varied but be varied in your mind
Before you hear the eventual return sound.

Play me the dance you made for the barge-master.
Stop stop Karl. Play it as you first thought
Of it in the hot boat-kitchen. That is a pleasure
For me. I can see I am making you good.
Keep the stove red. Hand me the matches. Now
We can see better. Give me a shot at the pipe.
Karl, I can still put on a good flute-mouth
And show you in this high cold room something
You will be famous to have said you heard.

The Fourth Lesson

You are early this morning. What we have to do
Today is think of you as a little creator
After the big creator. And it can be argued
You are as necessary, even a composer
Composing in the flesh an attitude
To slay the ears of the gentry. Karl,

I know you find great joy in the great
Composers. But now you can put your lips to
The messages and blow them into sound
And enter and be there as well. You must
Be faithful to who you are speaking from
And yet it is all right. You will be there.

Take your coat off. Sit down. A glass of Bols
Will help us both. I think you are good enough
To not need me anymore. I think you know
You are not only an interpreter.
What you will do is always something else
And they will hear you simultaneously with
The Art you have been given to read. Karl,

I think the Spring is really coming at last.
I see the canal boys working. I realise
I have not asked you to play the flute today.
Come and look. Are the barges not moving?
You must forgive me. I am not myself today.
Be here on Thursday. When you come, bring
Me five herrings. Watch your fingers. Spring
Is apparent but it is still chilblain weather.

The Last Lesson

Dear Karl, this morning is our last lesson.
I have been given the opportunity to
Live in a certain person's house and tutor
Him and his daughters on the traverse flute.
Karl, you will be all right. In those recent
Lessons my heart lifted to your playing.

I know. I see you doing well, invited
In a great chamber in front of the gentry. I
Can see them with their dresses settling in
And bored mouths beneath moustaches sizing
You up as you are, a lout from the canal
With big ears but an angel's tread on the flute.

But you will be all right. Stand in your place
Before them. Remember Johann. Begin with good
Nerve and decision. Do not intrude too much
Into the message you carry and put out.

One last thing, Karl, remember when you enter
The joy of those quick high archipelagoes,
To make to keep your finger-stops as light
As feathers but definite. What can I say more?
Do not be sentimental or in your Art.
I will miss you. Do not expect applause.

How are the Children Robin

for Robin Skelton

It does not matter how are you how are
The children flying leaving home so early?
The song is lost asleep the blackthorn breaks
Into its white flourish. The poet walks
At all odd times hoping the road is empty.
I mean me walking hoping the road is empty.

Not that I would ever expect to see
Them over the brow of the hill coming
In scarlet anoraks to meet their Dad.
A left, a right, my mad feet trudge the road
Between the busy times. It raineth now
Across the hedges and beneath the bough.

It does not matter let that be a lesson
To cross the fields. Keep off the road. The Black
Wood of Madron with its roof of rooks
Is lost asleep flying into the dusk.
When shall we see the children older returning
Into the treetops? And what are they bringing?

To My Wife at Midnight

I

Are you to say goodnight
And turn away under
The blanket of your delight?

Are you to let me go
Alone to sleep beside you
Into the drifting snow?

Where we each reach,
Sleeping alone together,
Nobody can touch.

Is the cat's window open?
Shall I turn into your back?
And what is to happen?

What is to happen to us
And what is to happen to each
Of us asleep in our places?

2

I mean us both going
Into sleep at our ages
To sleep and get our fairing.

They have all gone home.
Night beasts are coming out.
The black wood of Madron

Is just waking up.
I hear the rain outside
To help me to go to sleep.

Nessie, don't let my soul
Skip and miss a beat
And cause me to fall.

3

Are you asleep I say
Into the back of your neck
For you not to hear me.

Are you asleep? I hear
Your heart under the pillow
Saying my dear my dear

My dear for all it's worth.
Where is the dun's moor
Which began your breath?

4

Ness, to tell you the truth
I am drifting away
Down to fish for the saithe.

Is the cat's window open?
The weather is on my shoulder
And I am drifting down

Into O can you hear me
Among your Dunsmuir Clan?
Are you coming out to play?

5

Did I behave badly
On the field at Culloden?
I lie sore-wounded now

By all activities, and
The terrible acts of my time
Are only a distant sound.

With responsibility
I am drifting off
Breathing regularly

Into my younger days
To play the games of Greenock
Beside the sugar-house quays.

6

Nessie Dunsmuir, I say
Wheesht wheesht to myself
To help me now to go

Under into somewhere
In the redcoat rain.
Buckle me for the war.

Are you to say goodnight
And kiss me and fasten
My drowsy armour tight?

My dear camp-follower,
Hap the blanket round me
And tuck in a flower.

Maybe from my sleep
In the stoure at Culloden
I'll see you here asleep

In your lonely place.

NOTES

GIGHA

Gigha: an island off the Scottish coast, between Kintyre and Islay.

LISTEN PUT ON MORNING

This poem makes a number of oblique rhythmic allusions to Blake.
Graham enjoins us to listen while Blake enjoins us to see.

YOURS TRULY

This verse letter answers one Graham wrote about a quarter of a
century before, 'Letter VII'. 'Yours Truly' looks back at the experience of a passion that broke language:

My love, my love anywhere
Drifted away, listen.
From the dark rush under
Us comes our end. Endure
Each word as it breaks at last
To become our home here.
Who hears us now? Suddenly
In a stark flash the nerves
Of language broke. The sea
Cried out loud under the keel.
Listen. Now as I fall.

Listen. And silence even
Has turned away. Listen.

'Letter VII' (and the six other letters in the sequence) are a kind of axis in Graham's work, marking the culmination of earlier themes and style and pointing forward to such work as 'To My Wife at Midnight' and the more intense and complex because less *complicated* later poems. In 'Yours Truly' Graham humorously suggests that the earlier letter was 'too confused for words', though it was – and remains – 'new'. In the sequence of letters *Mooney* (later Malcolm Mooney), a frequent voice in Graham's work, made his first definitive appearance.

THE THERMAL STAIR

In gliding, the skill is to navigate the plane from thermal to thermal which, due to temperature and topography, is rising (as up stairs).

The place-names, names of houses and lighthouses, etc., refer to actual locations in and about Madron where Lanyon and Graham lived. The references to the local pubs, the domino player, etc., are all literal. Graham appropriates the Madron landscape much as Sisson does Somerset.

the jasper sea echoes a familiar Methodist hymn (a reference later developed in the poem).

alfred wallis: a 'naïve' painter of great humour and subtlety, a mutual acquaintance of Graham and Lanyon and one who shared their landscape.

Saracinesco: one of Lanyon's pictures.

the phallic boys: lighthouses and buoys.

Duchy shire: a reference to Cornwall's unique official status.

JOHANN JOACHIM QUANTZ'S FIVE LESSONS

Quantz was flute master to King Frederick of Prussia, a composer and a virtuoso player with tremendous influence at court. Quantz's chief requisites were 'a singable and interesting melody, deep feeling and, most important of all, "correctness".' Quantz wrote a classical manual on the flute and flute-playing. Graham's Quantz bears a somewhat threadbare relationship to his literal prototype. He is a genius fallen on hard times, no longer a court favourite but in his isolation refined into a remarkable disciplining teacher with an ear (and a respect) for genius in others. The poem, of course, is more than a character sketch and its theme embraces more than musical creation and performance.

TO MY WIFE AT MIDNIGHT

The poet's wife is Nessie Dunsmuir: her surname provides some of the puns and strengthens the historical allusions. The poem, referring to the battle of Culloden of 1746 (that marked the turn in fortunes of Prince Charles), hyperbolizes a domestic conflict with tender and ironic intent in the apology.

stoure: battle or combat, used figuratively to refer to 'a conflict waged with immaterial weapons; a struggle with pain or adversity'.

Donald Davie

Donald Alfred Davie was born in Barnsley, Yorkshire, in 1922. After military service he went to Cambridge and took his degree in English. He lectured in Dublin (1950–57), Cambridge (1958–64) and became Professor of English at Essex (1964). In 1968 he emigrated to the United States and became Professor of English at Stanford University and – in 1978 – at Vanderbilt. He still manages to spend several months of every year in Britain, and most of his verse and prose writing is addressed to a British audience.

Davie began his poetic career in the thick of The Movement, and although he grew well beyond it, his critical book, *Purity of Diction in English Verse* (1952), has been regarded as a kind of extended manifesto of the aspirations of the group. It was a reaction against the excesses of the poets of Dylan Thomas's generation and persuasion, but also a positive reassertion of the validity of syntactical clarity, traditional forms, and reason. As Davie wrote, 'there is no necessary connection between the poetic vocation on the one hand, and on the other exhibitionism, egoism, and licence'. For Davie, the rules of the early Movement were a discipline and not a dogma. His temperament is Augustan, didactic, normative. As his sense of social and poetic realities has changed, so his poetry has developed, and with it his criticism. He has come to accept that for a twentieth-century poet to yearn for Augustan precision and clarity is a form of romanticism. This recognition has had consequences for his work, for he suspects romanticism however it conceals itself. His translations of Pasternak and his reading in depth of Ezra Pound have further matured his thought and his own verse.

If Graham's dominant theme is language as an element through and in which the poet moves, taking his liberties where he can, Davie's dominant theme is language as a possession and a discipline, something which the poet controls, purifies, keeps to its meanings. The sin against language is the worst sin, for a cheapened and imprecise language diminishes communication, liberty, identity. Language is a civic and spiritual currency which it is the poet's task to see is not devalued. The poet is a deliberate creator, clarifying ideas, feelings and processes of thought.

Donald Davie's collections include *Brides of Reason* (1955), *A Winter Talent and Other Poems* (1957), *The Forests of Lithuania* (1959), *New and Selected Poems* (1961), *Events and Wisdoms: Poems 1957–1963* (1964), *Essex Poems* (1969), *Six Epistles to Eva Hesse* (1970), *Collected Poems 1950–1970* (1972), *The Shires* (1974) and *In The Stopping Train* (1977). His major sequence, *Three for Watermusic*, appeared in *PN Review 9* (1979).

In a way, Davie attempts to address a rational and literate 'reading public' in the Augustan sense. His knowledge of the fact that such a public does not now, or not yet, exist, has led to poems of acute self-questioning. As a didactic poet, he is often harsh and uncompromising in his truth-telling. But he is equally harsh with himself. His art is a discipline as well as a pleasure. He has had the remarkable skill to redirect his poetic energies, as it were, in mid-course, to recognize deficiencies in his early procedures as a poet and deliberately to remedy them. It is not surprising that he is among the finest critics of our time, as well as being a fine poet. A knowledge of his prose books, especially *Articulate Energy* (1955), *Ezra Pound: Poet as Sculptor* (1964), *Thomas Hardy and British Poetry* (1973) and *The Poet in the Imaginary Museum: Essays of Two Decades* (1977) enriches the understanding of his diverse talent.

Poem as Abstract

'To write about a tree . . . you must first be a tree.'
(W. R. RODGERS)

I

A poem is less an orange than a grid;
It hoists a charge; it does not ooze a juice.
It has no rind, being entirely hard.

All drumming yards and open, it asserts
That clouds have way upon them, and that hills
Breast into time behind a singing strut.

71

A sheer abstraction, apt upon the grass
Of London parks, has emulated oak
And aped the ramage that it could surpass.

That construct, ribbed with wire across a quern,
Is caging such serenity of stress
As boughs, or fruit that breaks them, cannot learn.

For gods are gathered from the styles they wear,
And do they curl, a foetus in a fruit,
Or, like Orion, pinned upon the air?

II

No trowelled matron but a rigger's mate,
The pile-high poet has no time to brood.
He steps the mast; it does not germinate.

Not for ingestion but to frame the air
He flies the spar that even winter's tree
In green ambition cannot grow so spare.

The orange dangles, drops, and comes again.
To make a fruit he has to be a fruit,
A globe of pulp about a pip of pain.

But tip-toe cages lofted in a day
(To make a grid he has to *make* a grid)
Have come unprecedented, and to stay.

If poems make a style, a way of walking
With enterprise, should not a poet's gait
Be counties-wide, this stride, the pylons stalking?

Remembering the 'Thirties

I

Hearing one saga, we enact the next.
We please our elders when we sit enthralled;
But then they're puzzled; and at last they're vexed
To have their youth so avidly recalled.

It dawns upon the veterans after all
That what for them were agonies, for us
Are high-brow thrillers, though historical;
And all their feats quite strictly fabulous.

This novel written fifteen years ago,
Set in my boyhood and my boyhood home,
These poems about 'abandoned workings', show
Worlds more remote than Ithaca or Rome.

The Anschluss, Guernica — all the names
At which those poets thrilled or were afraid
For me mean schools and schoolmasters and games;
And in the process some-one is betrayed.

Ourselves perhaps. The Devil for a joke
Might carve his own initials on our desk,
And yet we'd miss the point because he spoke
An idiom too dated, Audenesque.

Ralegh's Guiana also killed his son.
A pretty pickle if we came to see
The tallest story really packed a gun,
The Telemachiad an Odyssey.

II

Even to them the tales were not so true
As not to be ridiculous as well;
The ironmaster met his Waterloo,
But Rider Haggard rode along the fell.

'Leave for Cape Wrath tonight!' They lounged away
On Fleming's trek or Isherwood's ascent.
England expected every man that day
To show his motives were ambivalent.

They played the fool, not to appear as fools
In time's long glass. A deprecating air
Disarmed, they thought, the jeers of later schools;
Yet irony itself is doctrinaire,

And curiously, nothing now betrays
Their type to time's derision like this coy
Insistence on the quizzical, their craze
For showing Hector was a mother's boy.

73

A neutral tone is nowadays preferred.
And yet it may be better, if we must,
To praise a stance impressive and absurd
Than not to see the hero for the dust.

For courage is the vegetable king,
The sprig of all ontologies, the weed
That beards the slag-heap with his hectoring,
Whose green adventure is to run to seed.

Time Passing, Beloved

Time passing, and the memories of love
Coming back to me, carissima, no more mockingly
Than ever before; time passing, unslackening,
Unhastening, steadily; and no more
Bitterly, beloved, the memories of love
Coming into the shore.

How will it end? Time passing and our passages of love
As ever, beloved, blind
As ever before; time binding, unbinding
About us; and yet to remember
Never less chastening, nor the flame of love
Less like an ember.

What will become of us? Time
Passing, beloved, and we in a sealed
Assurance unassailed
By memory. How can it end,
This siege of a shore that no misgivings have steeled,
No doubts defend?

Dream Forest

These have I set up,
Types of ideal virtue,
To be authenticated
By no one's Life and Times,
But by a sculptor's logic

Of whom I have commanded,
To dignify my groves,
Busts in the antique manner,
Each in the space mown down
Under its own sway:

First, or to break the circle,
Brutus, imperious, curbed
Not much by the general will,
But by a will to be curbed,
A preference for limits;

Pushkin next, protean
Who recognised no checks
Yet brooked them all – a mind
Molten and thereby fluent,
Unforced, easily strict;

The next, less fortunate,
Went honourably mad,
The angry annalist
Of hearth and marriage bed,
Strindberg – a staring head.

Classic, romantic, realist,
These have I set up.
These have I set, and a few trees.
When will a grove grow over
This mile upon mile of moor?

The Wearing of the Green

Gold is not autumn's privilege;
A tawny ripening
In Meath in May burns ready in the hedge;
The yellow that will follow spring
Accentuates its wet and green array,
A sumptuous trill beneath
The shriller edge
Of Meath in May.

Green more entire must needs be evergreen,
Precluding autumn and this spring
Of Meath in May, its in-between
Of golds and yellows preluding
The liquid summer. Must the seasons stay
Their temperate career because
A flag is green
In Meath in May?

Imagination, Irish avatar,
Aches in the spring's heart and in mine, the stranger's,
In Meath in May. But to believe there are
Unchanging Springs endangers,
By that fast dye, the earth;
So blood-red green the season,
It never changes
In Meath in May.

A Winter Talent

Lighting a spill late in the afternoon,
I am that coal whose heat it should unfix;
Winter is come again, and none too soon
For meditation on its raft of sticks.

Some quick bright talents can dispense with coals
And burn their boats continually, command
An unreflecting brightness that unrolls
Out of whatever firings come to hand.

What though less sunny spirits never turn
The dry detritus of an August hill
To dangerous glory? Better still to burn
Upon that gloom where all have felt a chill.

Heigh-ho on a Winter Afternoon

There is a heigh-ho in these glowing coals
By which I sit wrapped in my overcoat
As if for a portrait by Whistler. And there is
A heigh-ho in the bird that noiselessly

76

Flew just now past my window, to alight
On winter's moulding, snow; and an alas,
A heigh-ho and a desultory chip,
Chip, chip on stone from somewhere down below.

Yes I have 'mellowed', as you said I would,
And that's a heigh-ho too for any man;
Heigh-ho that means we fall short of alas
Which sprigs the grave of higher hopes than ours.
Yet heigh-ho too has its own luxuries,
And salts with courage to be jocular
Disreputable sweets of wistfulness,
By depreciation made presentable.

What should we do to rate the long alas
But skeeter down a steeper gradient?
And then some falls are still more fortunate,
The meteors spent, the tragic heroes stunned
Who go out like a light. But here the chip,
Chip, chip will flake the stone by slow degrees,
For hour on hour the fire will gutter down,
The bird will call at longer intervals.

With the Grain

I

Why, by an ingrained habit, elevate
    Into their own ideas
Activities like carpentry, become
    The metaphors of graining?
Gardening, the one word, tilth? Or thought,
    The idea of having ideas,
Resolved into images of tilth and graining?

An ingrained habit . . . This is fanciful:
    And there's the rub
Bristling, where the irritable block
    Screams underneath the blade
Of love's demand, or in crimped and gouged-out
    Shavings only, looses
Under a peeling logic its perceptions.

Language (mine, when wounding,
    Yours, back-biting) lacks
No whorl nor one-way shelving. It resists,
    Screams its remonstrance, planes
Reluctantly to a level. And the most
    Reasonable of settlements betrays
Unsmoothed resentment under the caress.

II

The purest hue, let only the light be sufficient
    Turns colour. And I was told
If painters frequent St Ives
    It is because the light
There, under the cliff, is merciful. I dream
    Of an equable light upon words
And as painters paint in St Ives, the poets speaking.

Under that cliff we should say, my dear,
    Not what we mean, but what
The words would mean. We should speak,
    As carpenters work,
With the grain of our words. We should utter
    Unceasingly the hue of love
Safe from the battery of changeable light.

(Love, a condition of such fixed colour,
    Cornwall indeed, or Wales
Might foster. Lovers in mauve,
    Like white-robed Druids
Or the Bards in blue, would need
    A magical philtre, no less,
Like Iseult's, to change partners.)

III

Such a fourth estate of the realm,
    Hieratic unwinking
Mauve or blue under skies steel-silver,
    Would chamfer away
A knot in the grain of a streaming light, the glitter,
    Off lances' points, that moved
A sluggish Froissart to aesthetic feeling.

78

And will the poet, carpenter of light,
    Work with the grain henceforward?
If glitterings won't fetch him
    Nor the refractory crystal,
Will he never again look into the source of light
    Aquiline, but fly
Always out of the sun, unseen till softly alighting?

Why, by an ingrained habit, elevate
    Into the light of ideas
The colourful trades, if not like Icarus
    To climb the beam? High lights
Are always white, but this ideal sun
    Dyes only more intensely, and we find
Enough cross-graining in the most abstract nature.

A Lily at Noon

Deep-sea frost, and
Lilies at noon . . .
Late leaves, late leaves
Toss every day.
The daymoon shines always for some.
In the marriage of a slow man
Eighteen years is soon.

Sun and moon, no
Dark between,
Foresight and hindsight
Halving the hours.
And now he collects his thoughts
Before it is too late.
But what can 'too late' mean?

Shielding with hands,
Binding to stakes . . .
Late leaves, late leaves
Toss every day,
The sun moves on from noon.
To freeze, to cup, to retard –
These measures terror takes.

Rodez

Northward I came, and knocked in the coated wall
At the door of a low inn scaled like a urinal
With greenish tiles. The door gave, and I came

Home to the stone north, every wynd and snicket
Known to me wherever the flattened cat
Squirmed home to a hole between housewall and paving.

Known! And in the turns of it, no welcome,
No flattery of the beckoned lighted eye
From a Rose of the rose-brick alleys of Toulouse.

Those more than tinsel garlands, more than masks,
Unfading wreaths of ancient summers, I
Sternly cast off. A stern eye is the graceless

Bulk and bruise that at the steep uphill
Confronts me with its drained-of-colour sandstone
Implacably. The Church. It is Good Friday.

Goodbye to the Middle Ages! Although some
Think that I enter them, those centuries
Of monkish superstition, here I leave them

With their true garlands, and their honest masks,
Every fresh flower cast on the porch and trodden,
Raked by the wind at the Church door on this Friday.

Goodbye to all the centuries. There is
No home in them, much as the dip and turn
Of an honest alley charmingly deceive us.

And yet not quite goodbye. Instead almost
Welcome, I said. Bleak equal centuries
Crowded the porch to be deflowered, crowned.

July, 1964

I smell a smell of death.
Roethke, who died last year
with whom I drank in London,
wrote the book I am reading;
a friend, of a firm mind,
has died or is dying now,
a telegram informs me;
the wife of a neighbour died
in three quick months of cancer.

Love and art I practise;
they seem to be worth no more
and no less than they were.
The firm mind practised neither.
It practised charity
vocationally and
yet for the most part truly.
Roethke, who practised both,
was slack in his art by the end.

The practise of an art
is to convert all terms
into the terms of art.
By the end of the third stanza
death is a smell no longer;
it is a problem of style.
A man who ought to know me
wrote in a review
my emotional life was meagre.

January

Arable acres heave
Mud and a few bare trees
Behind St Michael's
Kirby le Soken, where
The pew I share
Promises the vicinity I leave.

Diatribe and
Denunciation, where
I spend my days,
Populous townships, sink
Into the haze that lowers
Over my neighbour's land.

Resignation, oh winter tree
At peace, at peace . . .
Read it what way you will,
A wish that fathers. In a field between
The Sokens, Thorpe and Kirby, stands
A bare Epiphany.

A Winter Landscape
near Ely

It is not life being short,
Death certain, that is making
Those faintly coffee-coloured
Gridiron marks on the snow
Or that row of trees heart-breaking.

What stirs us when a curtain
Of ice-hail dashes the window?
It is the wasteness of space
That a man drives wagons into
Or plants his windbreak in.

Spaces stop time from hurting.
Over verst on verst of Russia
Are lime-tree avenues.

Epistle. To Enrique Caracciolo Trejo

(Essex)

A shrunken world
Stares from my pages.
What a pellet the authentic is!
My world of poetry,
Enrique, is not large.
Day by day it is smaller.
These poems that you have
Given me, I might
Have made them English once.

Now they are inessential.
The English that I feel in
Fears the inauthentic
Which invades it on all sides
Mortally. The style may die of it,
Die of the fear of it,
Confounding authenticity with essence.

Death, an authentic subject,
Jaime Sabinès has
Dressed with the yew-trees of funereal trope.
It cannot be his fault
If the English that I feel in
Feels itself too poor
Spirited to plant a single cypress.
It is afraid of showing, at the grave-side,
Its incapacity to venerate
Life, or the going of it. These are deaths,
These qualms and horrors shade the ancestral ground.

Sabinès in another
Poem comes down
To the sound of pigeons on a neighbour's tiles,
A manifest of gladness.
Such a descent on clapping wings the English
Contrives to trust

No longer. My own garden
Crawls with a kind of obese
Pigeon from Belgium; they burst through cracking branches
Like frigate-birds.

Still in infested gardens
The year goes round,
A smiling landscape greets returning Spring.
To see what can be said for it, on what
Secure if shallow ground
Of feeling England stands
Unshaken for
Her measure to be taken
Has taken four bad years
Of my life here. And now
I know the ground:
Humiliation, corporate and private,
Not chastens but chastises
This English and this verse.

I cannot abide the new
Absurdities day by day,
The new adulterations.
I relish your condition,
Expatriate! though it be among
A people whose constricted idiom
Cannot embrace the poets you thought to bring them.

Rousseau in His Day

So many nights the solitary lamp had burned;
So many nights his lone mind, slowing down
Deliberately, had questioned, as it turned
Mooning upon its drying stem, what arc
Over a lifetime day had moved him through.

Always he hoped he might deserve a Plutarch,
Not to be one posterity forgot.
Nor have we. He has left his mark: one tight
Inched-around circuit of the screw of light,
As glowing shadows track the life of roses
Over unchosen soil-crumbs. It was not
What he'd expected or the world supposes.

Portland

after Pasternak

Portland, the Isle of Portland – how I love
Not the place, its name! It is as if
These names were your name, and the cliff, the breaking
Of waves along a reach of tumbled stone
Were a configuration of your own
Firm slopes and curves – your clavicles, your shoulder.
A glimpse of that can set the hallway shaking.

And I am a night sky that is tired of shining,
Tired of its own hard brilliance, and I sink.

Tomorrow morning, grateful, I shall seem
Keen, but be less clear-headed than I think;
A brightness more than clarity will sail
Off lips that vapour formulations, make
Clear sound, full rhyme, and rational order take
Account of a dream, a sighing cry, a moan,

Like foam on all three sides at midnight lighting
Up, far off, a seaward jut of stone.

Grudging Respect

As when a ruined face
Lifted among those crowding
For the young squire's largesse
Perceives him recognize
Her and she grabs, not for any
Languidly lofted penny
They scrabble for, but for his eyes
And pockets them, their clouding
That instant; and the abruptness
With which his obliging is checked,
His suddenly leaving the place . . .

Just so may a grudging respect
Be, from a despised one,
Not just better than none
At all, but sweeter than any.

The Fountain of Cyane

Her father's brother rapes her!
          In the bright
Ovidian colours all is for delight,
The inadmissible minglings are recounted
With such finesse: the beery ram that mounted
His niece and, hissing 'Belt up', had her, is
Hell's grizzly monarch gaunt in tapestries;
The thrashing pallid skivvy under him
A vegetation myth; the stinking slum
Is Enna's field where Phoebus ne'er invades
The tufted fences, nor offends the shades;
And her guffawing Ma assumes the land,
Coarsely divine, cacophonous, gin in hand
Sky-blue, dark-blue, sea-green, cerulean dyes
Dye into fables what we'd hoped were lies
And feared were truths. A happy turn, a word,
Says they are both, and nothing untoward.
Coloured by rhetoric, to die of grief
Becomes as graceful as a falling leaf;
No chokings, retchings, not the same as dying
Starved and worn out because you can't stop crying.
Cyane's fable, that one; how she wept
Herself away, shocked for her girl-friend raped –
'Her varied members to a fluid melt,
A pliant softness in her bones is felt . . .'
Sweet lapse, sweet lapse . . . 'till only now remains
Within the channel of her purple veins
A silver liquor . . .' Ah, the master's touch
So suave, mere word-play, that can do so much!
And now at last imperious, in bad taste:
'Nothing to fill love's grasp; her husband chaste
Bathes in that bosom he before embrac'd.'

The spring-fed pool that is Cyane may
Be visited in Sicily today;
And what's to be made of that? Or how excuse
Our intent loitering outside Syracuse?

86

2

Modesty, I kept saying,
Temperate, temperate . . . Yes,
The papyrus were swaying
Hardly at all, and late,
Late in the season the rings
Widened upon the reedy
Pool, and the beady-eyed frogs
Volleyed out after mayfly.

Fountain? No jet, no spume,
Spew nor spurt . . . Was this
Where Pluto's chariot hurtled
Up out of 'gloomy Dis'?
Male contumely for that
First most seminal rape,
Proserpine's, prescribes
Some more vertiginous landscape.

Late, late in that season . . .
Easy, easy the lap
And rustle of blue waters . . .
Wholly a female occasion
This, as Demeter launches
One fish in a silver arc
To signalize her daughter's
Re-entry to the dark.

3

The balked, the aborted vision
Permits of the greater finesse;
The achieved one is fugitive, slighter,
One might almost say, 'loose'.

And yet the oceanic
Swells of an unencumbered
Metric jiggle the planes
Epiphanies must glow from.

So, though one might almost say 'loose',
One mustn't. They like the closed-off
Precincts all right, but never
When those exult in their closures.

The shrine is enclosed from the bare
Fields and, three miles away
Clearly in sight, the high-rise
Shimmering haze of the city.

But the fence is of wire; the warped
Palings give easy access;
No turnstile; and at the pool
Of Cyane, nothing to pay;

No veil to be rent, no grille,
No holy of holies. The Greek
World, one is made to remember,
Was Christianized quite early.

Epiphanies all around us
Always perhaps. And some
Who missed the flash of a fin
Were keeping their eyes on rhyme-schemes.

4

And so with stanzas . . . moving
From room to room is a habit adapted to winter,
Warm and warming, worship Sunday by Sunday,
And one is glad of it. But when,
Now and again I turn the knob and enter
The special chill where my precarious Springs
Hang water-beaded in still air, I hear
A voice announce: 'And this is the
Conservatory!' Greenish misted panes
Of mystifying memory conserve
In an unnatural silence nymph and pool;
It is an outside room, at the end of a range of rooms
But still a room, accounted for or even
Entered upon the impatient plans in my
Infidel youth. At that time no
Nymph, and no pool: still, it appears,
Room left for them – and yet
Rooms should have an outside door, I think;
I wilt for lack of it, though my plants do not.

5

Yet there was enough in this –
And it was nothing, nothing at all
'Happened' – enough in this
Non-happening to cap
What Scripture says of the Fall

Which, though it equally may
Not in that sense have happened, is
A postulate day by day
Called for, to explain
Our joys, our miseries.

A fish jumped, silver; small
Frogs took the mayfly; papyrus
In the Sicilian fall
Of the leaf was bowing. How
That weightless weighed with us!

Why, when an unheard air
Stirred in the fronds, did we assume
An occidental care
For proximate cause? Egyptian
Stems abased their plume.

So inattentive we are
We think ourselves unfallen. This
Pool, when Pluto's car
Whirled up, was wept by Cyane
For her abducted mistress.

One could go round and round
This single and Sicilian less
Than happening, and ground
Therein what might suffuse
Our lives with happiness.

NOTES

POEM AS ABSTRACT

The epigraph is from William Robert Rodgers (1909–68), the Ulster poet. Davie dissents from Rodgers's prescription here and (in prose) in *Articulate Energy* (1955, pp. 13 and 19), referring to Rodgers's article 'Speak and Span' (*New Statesman*, 15 December 1951, p. 704). This poem is part of Davie's definition of syntax in poetry, its potentialities, and the sorts of ends it can be turned to.

REMEMBERING THE 'THIRTIES

Originally, the poem bore an epigraph from Paul Tillich: 'Courage is an ethical reality, but it is rooted in the whole breadth of existence and ultimately in the structure of being itself.' It is an irony that does not escape Davie that Ithaca and Rome require no footnote, while allusions from very recent history are obscure to many.

Anschluss: the union of Germany and Austria between the two World Wars, paving the way for the Second of them.

Guernica: a town in northern Spain, seat of the Basque parliament during the Civil War, bombed by German planes in 1937 on behalf of General Franco; subject of a well-known painting by Pablo Picasso.

For the young Davie, even the voice of W. H. Auden (author of the 'poems about "abandoned workings"' in line 11) seems remote, though Auden was the representative voice – ideologically and poetically – of the 1930s, especially with reference to the Spanish Civil War. The immediate past is alien, while in the more distant past events have considerable integrity and resonance.

Ralegh's Guiana: Sir Walter Raleigh – historian, naval commander, courtier and (incidentally) poet (1552–1618) – lost his son in his final abortive expedition to Guiana.

The Telemachiad an Odyssey suggests that the classical order of events is altered: in Homer's *Odyssey*, the narrative begins with the son, Telemachus, seeking his father (a *Telemachiad*); but the father's story is the purpose of the poem. Now, Telemachus's adventures become an Odyssey in themselves. The father, or the earlier generation and its concerns, are lost sight of.

Sir Henry Rider Haggard (1856–1925), the novelist, was best-known for his romances *King Solomon's Mines* (1885) and *She* (1887).

Robert Peter Fleming (b. 1907) was a journalist and travel writer.

Christopher Isherwood (b. 1904), the novelist and a friend of Auden's, collaborated with the poet in several projects, three of them plays (the allusion here is to *The Ascent of F.6*, 1937). The political uncertainty of the period meant that England could no longer 'expect' selfless sacrifice from her citizens. The individual (especially the intellectual individual) citizen was ideologically torn. His strategy was likely to be ironic and self-conscious. But his very ambivalence dates him and limits the value of his work. A continuity is broken, values are questioned.

Hector, the Trojan hero whose defeat by Achilles hastened the Trojan defeat, is traduced into an effeminate figure. The hero was no longer one who defended his city but the one who, at a time of crisis, stood back to criticize it. Such a 'neutral tone' – modish and often facile – came to dominate. Davie expresses his own reluctant admiration for those whose stance was in a more antique manner. The poem begins the articulation of a political credo Davie's later work has clarified and extended.

TIME PASSING, BELOVED

carissima: dearest.

DREAM FOREST

The structure recalls W. B. Yeats's poem 'In Memory of Major Robert Gregory'. Here, the three figures – a political figure, a poet, and a dramatist, each distinctly exemplary – from three periods, represent valid modes of intense vision, three choices for the writer.

THE WEARING OF THE GREEN

Despite the effectively accentual prosody of this poem, it may strike the reader as an oblique tribute to the poetry of Thomas Hardy. Its point of reference is Ireland (where the poet lived and taught) and there is implicit in it an eloquent civicism, an awareness of Irish history in the Irish landscape.

WITH THE GRAIN

In the notes to his *Collected Poems*, Davie calls this poem 'obscure' and relates it to a diary entry written shortly before in which he had reflected that he was 'not a poet by nature, only by inclination' – he found it easier to express ideas than experiences. He confesses that he lacked 'the poet's need of concreteness'. His earlier poems might have been expressed in non-poetic forms. He resolves to write differently in future, 'only poems which are, if not *naturally*, at all events *truly* poems throughout', working 'against the grain', 'towards the concrete'. This poem is among the first fruits of this resolve.

St Ives: in Cornwall, much frequented by artists.

The allusion to *Iseult* (Isolde) is particularly apposite to setting and theme since it was to a Cornish harbour that she was bound.

Jean Froissart (1337?–1410?) wrote the *Chroniques*, an account of European events whose considerable literary merit is not matched with historical accuracy; nonetheless, it vividly evokes courtly life.

Icarus: attempting to fly, he made wings of wax and feathers but ascended too high: his wings were melted by the sun and he fell into the sea.

RODEZ

The title refers to the circular movement of the poem and the theme of home-coming or return, relating also to the annual re-enactment of the Crucifixion (it is Good Friday) and to the formally different but radically similar faiths of the South (Roman Catholic) and North (here Methodist). The North is evoked in its own idiom (*wynd and snicket*: alleys and narrow passages) and contrasts with the sensually exciting South. The North, with its harsh climate and short history, lacks the body and richness of the South: the returning poet feels its poverty, the way it absorbs and renders contourless centuries of history in its architectural and spiritual areas of denial. (Compare this poem with R. S. Thomas's 'Pavane'.)

JULY, 1964

Roethke: Theodore Roethke (1908–63), the American poet, whose best book was *The Lost Son and other poems* (1948). The poem relates to Davie's essay 'Two Ways Out of Whitman' (1964) reprinted in *The Poet in the Imaginary Museum: Essays of Two Decades*. Davie's suggestion that Roethke's later work marked a 'falling off' is just. Admirers of the cumulative rhetoric of Roethke's late work are ill at ease with the scrupulous economy of Davie's work and confuse his practice of an art that aims at truth with mere artifice or heartlessness.

EPISTLE. TO ENRIQUE CARACCIOLO TREJO

Trejo, the Spanish-language poet and essayist, tried to interest Davie in certain Latin-American poets when he was at Essex.

Jaime Sabinès: (b. 1925), the Mexican poet who in his earlier work contrasts the simplicity of provincial life with the corruption of the capital.

DONALD DAVIE

ROUSSEAU IN HIS DAY

Jean-Jacques Rousseau (1712–1778), the French writer.

Plutarch: the first-century Greek biographer and moral philosopher. Rousseau in his *Confessions* proved his own Plutarch, revealing his character with great candour and not always in a creditable light.

PORTLAND

The poem is based loosely on one by the Russian poet *Boris Pasternak* (1890–1960), whom Davie translated and on whom he has written critically. The Isle of Portland, off the Dorset coast, becomes the pretext for one of Davie's finest love-poems.

THE FOUNTAIN OF CYANE

This is the first poem in the sequence *Three for Watermusic*, perhaps Davie's finest work to date. Conceptually it owes a debt to T. S. Eliot's *Four Quartets* (Eliot is a determining influence on Davie's work as he is, to distinct effect, on Sisson's).

Cyane is a spring in Sicily, near Arethusa, and the story of Cyane is told in Ovid's *Metamorphoses* V. It is told briefly in the context of the story of the rape of Proserpine, daughter of Demeter (the fertility goddess), who was snatched off to Hades by Pluto and in the end divided her time between her mother and her infernal lord (her stays in either place corresponded to summer and winter). The first section, based on translations by Dryden and his contemporaries, thriftily evokes Cyane's own tale, how she had dissolved into a pool in horror at her own act. There are also allusions (by quotation) to Milton. Davie introduced the poem in a radio broadcast and said: 'I must ask you to believe, what I assure you is true, that this grubbing about in ancient mythology wasn't the effective source of my poem but on the contrary was provoked only by an indisputable experience that I had, at a definite time in a definite place, there in Sicily.'

Philip Larkin

Philip Larkin was born in Coventry in 1922. He went to Oxford in the early 1940s. There he made the acquaintance of John Wain, Kingsley Amis, and others who were to be associated with The Movement (see p. 5). After Oxford, he became a university librarian and served at Belfast, Leicester, and finally at the Brynmor Jones Library in Hull.

His early verse, reprinted with an amusing and candid foreword by the poet in *The North Ship* (1945, reprinted 1974) showed the influence of Yeats and of Dylan Thomas to an extraordinary degree. A reading of the poetry of Hardy cured Larkin of his early infatuation with the romanticism of an earlier generation, and with *The Less Deceived* (1955) his distinctive talent appeared. His work was the centrepiece of The Movement anthology *New Lines* (1956). A fine writer in conventional forms, Larkin has not developed technically since the 1955 collection, except in the matter of deftness. His evolution in *The Whitsun Weddings* (1964) and *High Windows* (1974) has been thematic. There is a growing civic content in his poems, an always more lucid and generally pertinent perception of a landscape and a culture self-impoverished, losing touch with its rituals and its values. The voice is that of one who records and – in recording – suffers these impoverishments. Larkin's representative 'we' has given rise to the objection that he speaks very much of his own witness and perhaps of the witness and attitudes of his generation, but that the world he portrays is unnaturally bleak, that things are not as bad as he makes them out to be, and he seeks to bind us in unwilling complicity. But even his civic poetry has a strong personal content, and the pervasive sense of unfulfilment is typical of the experience of many readers. His verse is not limited by its chosen subject-matter.

94

One of Larkin's characteristic procedures is to describe a person or a type of person – or, indeed, a community – in terms of the things with which it surrounds itself. In 'Mr Bleaney' (p. 102), the absent Bleaney is evoked in the poor details of the room in which he stayed; in 'Here' (p. 101) a community is evoked by its landscape. The reader is left to deduce from detail – and the terms in which detail is presented – the character of the inhabitants of a place. The poet assists our deductions by his skilful handling of tone in traditional forms. He can be wry, elegiac, satirical, tender, ironic and self-deflating. His poems are memorable in whole or in part after a very few readings by virtue not only of his verbal skill but of his control of tone.

Larkin has written two novels: *Jill* (1946) and *A Girl in Winter* (1947). In 1973 his anthology *The Oxford Book of Twentieth-Century English Verse* appeared. He has written jazz criticism and occasional essays as well.

Many critics and polemicists distrust the effect Larkin's verse might have on younger writers. Taken apart from the alleged influence it is their misfortune to have foisted upon them, the best poems fully merit the acclaim they have earned. It is Larkin's fiction and his journalism that are more patently open to controversy: his rejection of modernism in its various forms, his distrust of imaginative enterprises more bold than his own. The quality of his writing, and his willingness to undertake the most difficult traditional forms and write in them about perennial themes, while using an idiom and a frame of reference strictly of our time, are in themselves a bold enterprise. His collected poems total fewer than 120, thirty-two of which he has republished on sufferance. He is a poet who writes when he must and when he can. Most of his poems in the three books of his maturity are excellent. The standard he has set himself is high: hence the scarcity of what he has passed for press.

Wedding-Wind

The wind blew all my wedding-day,
And my wedding-night was the night of the high wind;
And a stable door was banging, again and again,
That he must go and shut it, leaving me
Stupid in candlelight, hearing rain,
Seeing my face in the twisted candlestick,

The two underlined phrases indicate all is not as perfect as it may seem.

Yet seeing nothing. When he came back
He said the horses were restless, and I was sad
That any man or beast that night should lack
The happiness I had.

'He' is always going, she remains. Certain passivity in the female figure. Case of 'the lady protesteth too much.'

Now in the day
All's ravelled under the sun by the wind's blowing.
He has gone to look at the floods, and I
Carry a chipped pail to the chicken-run,
Set it down, and stare. All is the wind
Hunting through clouds and forests, thrashing
My apron and the hanging cloths on the line.

She is associated with the cloths and the apron. Hints of dissatisfaction

The wind She chooses as a symbol of her happiness but that too has negative points — It makes the horses restless and keeps humans awake.

Can it be borne, this bodying-forth by wind
Of joy my actions turn on, like a thread
Carrying beads? Shall I be let to sleep
Now this perpetual morning shares my bed?
Can even death dry up
These new delighted lakes, conclude
Our kneeling as cattle by all-generous waters?

Next, Please

Always too eager for the future, we
Pick up bad habits of expectancy.
Something is always approaching; every day
Till then we say,

Watching from a bluff the tiny, clear,
Sparkling armada of promises draw near.
How slow they are! And how much time they waste,
Refusing to make haste!

Yet still they leave us holding wretched stalks *Vivid image.*
Of disappointment, for though nothing balks *thwarts*
Each big approach, leaning with brasswork prinked,
Each rope distinct,

Flagged, and the figurehead with golden tits
Arching our way, it never anchors; it's
No sooner present than it turns to past.
Right to the last

We think each one will heave to and unload
All good into our lives, all we are owed
For waiting so devoutly and so long.
But we are wrong:

[handwritten: passivity- Larkin believes we have little control in our lives.]

Only one ship is seeking us, a black-
Sailed unfamiliar, towing at her back
A huge and birdless silence. In her wake
No waters breed or break.

[handwritten: vivid image.]

Going

There is an evening coming in
Across the fields, one never seen before,
That lights no lamps.

Silken it seems at a distance, yet
When it is drawn up over the knees and breast
It brings no comfort.

Where has the tree gone, that locked
Earth to the sky? What is under my hands,
That I cannot feel?

What loads my hands down?   *[handwritten: Death.]*

Wants

Beyond all this, the wish to be alone:
However the sky grows dark with invitation-cards
However we follow the printed directions of sex
However the family is photographed under the flagstaff –
Beyond all this, the wish to be alone.

Beneath it all, desire of oblivion runs:
Despite the artful tensions of the calendar,
The life insurance, the tabled fertility rites,
The costly aversion of the eyes from death –
Beneath it all, desire of oblivion runs.

[handwritten: We fill up our lives with all this crap to avert our eyes from death.]

Church Going

keeping him-self apart

Once I am sure there's nothing going on
I step inside, letting the door thud shut.
Another church: matting, seats, and stone,
And little books; sprawlings of flowers, cut
For Sunday, brownish now; some brass and stuff
Up at the holy end; the small neat organ;
And a tense, musty, unignorable silence,
Brewed God knows how long. Hatless, I take off
My cycle-clips in awkward reverence,

flippant tone-but is this genuine?

Move forward, run my hand around the font.
From where I stand, the roof looks almost new –
Cleaned, or restored? Someone would know: I don't.
Mounting the lectern, I peruse a few
Hectoring large-scale verses, and pronounce
'Here endeth' much more loudly than I'd meant.
The echoes snigger briefly. Back at the door
I sign the book, donate an Irish sixpence,
Reflect the place was not worth stopping for.

builds up picture of him as out of place - this is the image he wants to present.

Yet stop I did: in fact I often do,
And always end much at a loss like this,
Wondering what to look for; wondering, too,
When churches fall completely out of use
What we shall turn them into, if we shall keep
A few cathedrals chronically on show,
Their parchment, plate and pyx in locked cases,
And let the rest rent-free to rain and sheep.
Shall we avoid them as unlucky places?

There is some-thing indefinable which draws him to churches

So why does he stop?

chronically ill

vessel for the Eucharist

Superstition replaces religion until that too dies.

Or, after dark, will dubious women come
To make their children touch a particular stone;
Pick simples for a cancer; or on some
Advised night see walking a dead one?
Power of some sort or other will go on
In games, in riddles, seemingly at random;
But superstition, like belief, must die,
And what remains when disbelief has gone?
Grass, weedy pavement, brambles, buttress, sky,

the power

he traces disintegration of churches.

A shape less recognisable each week,
A purpose more obscure. I wonder who
Will be the last, the very last, to seek
This place for what it was; one of the crew
That tap and jot and know what rood-lofts were?   *ie even the religious are not really religious*
Some ruin-bibber, randy for antique,
Or Christmas-addict, counting on a whiff
Of gowns-and-bands and organ-pipes and myrrh?
Or will he be my representative,   *ie that churches mean nothing now.*

Bored, uninformed, knowing the ghostly silt   *fascination.*
Dispersed, yet tending to this cross of ground
Through suburb scrub because it held unspilt
So long and equably what since is found   *evenly/moderately*
Only in separation – marriage, and birth,   *ie not united within the church*
And death, and thoughts of these – for which was built
This special shell? For, though I've no idea
What this accoutred frowsty barn is worth,   *equipped, stuffy*
It pleases me to stand in silence here;

A serious house on serious earth it is,
In whose blent air all our compulsions meet,   *this is why it is fascinating. Lives are within the church.*
Are recognised, and robed as destinies.
And that much never can be obsolete,
Since someone will forever be surprising
A hunger in himself to be more serious,
And gravitating with it to this ground,
Which, he once heard, was proper to grow wise in,
If only that so many dead lie round.   *Throw away line, attempting to disguise his fascination a little.*

To play down its importance to him, this is what the persona tries to do throughout.

I Remember, I Remember

Coming up England by a different line
For once, early in the cold new year,
We stopped, and, watching men with number-plates
Sprint down the platform to familiar gates,
'Why, Coventry!' I exclaimed. 'I was born here.'

I leant far out, and squinnied for a sign
That this was still the town that had been 'mine'
So long, but found I wasn't even clear
Which side was which. From where those cycle-crates
Were standing, had we annually departed

It means nothing- we see that in the beginning- It isn't his hometown but 'where he was born.'

For all those family hols? . . . A whistle went:
Things moved. I sat back, staring at my boots.
'Was that,' my friend smiled, 'where you "have your roots"?'
No, only where my childhood was unspent, *negative tone begun which culminates in the last sentence.*
I wanted to retort, just where I started:

By now I've got the whole place clearly charted.
Our garden, first: where I did not invent
Blinding theologies of flowers and fruits,
And wasn't spoken to by an old hat.
And here we have that splendid family

I never ran to when I got depressed,
The boys all biceps and the girls all chest,
Their comic Ford, their farm where I could be
'Really myself'. I'll show you, come to that,
The bracken where I never trembling sat,

Determined to go through with it; where she
Lay back, and 'all became a burning mist'.
And, in those offices, my doggerel
Was not set up in blunt ten-point, nor read
By a distinguished cousin of the mayor,

Who didn't call and tell my father *There
Before us, had we the gift to see ahead* –
'You look as if you wished the place in Hell,'
My friend said, 'judging from your face.' 'Oh well,
I suppose it's not the place's fault,' I said.

'Nothing, like something, happens anywhere.'

At Grass

The eye can hardly pick them out
From the cold shade they shelter in,
Till wind distresses tail and mane;
Then one crops grass, and moves about
– The other seeming to look on –
And stands anonymous again.

Yet fifteen years ago, perhaps
Two dozen distances sufficed
To fable them: faint afternoons
Of Cups and Stakes and Handicaps,
Whereby their names were artificed
To inlay faded, classic Junes –

Silks at the start: against the sky
Numbers and parasols: outside,
Squadrons of empty cars, and heat,
And littered grass: then the long cry
Hanging unhushed till it subside
To stop-press columns on the street.

evocation of image

Do memories plague their ears like flies?
They shake their heads. Dusk brims the shadows.
Summer by summer all stole away,
The starting-gates, the crowds and cries –
All but the unmolesting meadows.
Almanacked, their names live; they

Have slipped their names, and stand at ease,
Or gallop for what must be joy,
And not a fieldglass sees them home,
Or curious stop-watch prophesies:
Only the groom, and the groom's boy,
With bridles in the evening come.

tone of envy – once they worked, now they are at rest. Humans don't have it this easy.

Here

Swerving east, from rich industrial shadows
And traffic all night north; swerving through fields
Too thin and thistled to be called meadows,
And now and then a harsh-named halt, that shields
Workmen at dawn; swerving to solitude
Of skies and scarecrows, haystacks, hares and pheasants,
And the widening river's slow presence,
The piled gold clouds, the shining gull-marked mud,

harsh images

sibilance

more pleasant, softer.

Gathers to the surprise of a large town:
Here domes and statues, spires and cranes cluster
Beside grain-scattered streets, barge-crowded water,
And residents from raw estates, brought down
The dead straight miles by stealing flat-faced trolleys,
Push through plate-glass swing doors to their desires –
Cheap suits, red kitchen-ware, sharp shoes, iced lollies,
Electric mixers, toasters, washers, driers –

A cut-price crowd, urban yet simple, dwelling
Where only salesmen and relations come
Within a terminate and fishy-smelling
Pastoral of ships up streets, the slave museum,
Tattoo-shops, consulates, grim head-scarfed wives;
And out beyond its mortgaged half-built edges
Fast-shadowed wheat-fields, running high as hedges,
Isolate villages, where removed lives

Loneliness clarifies. Here silence stands
Like heat. Here leaves unnoticed thicken,
Hidden weeds flower, neglected waters quicken,
Luminously-peopled air ascends;
And past the poppies bluish neutral distance
Ends the land suddenly beyond a beach
Of shapes and shingle. Here is unfenced existence:
Facing the sun, untalkative, out of reach.

Mr Bleaney

'This was Mr Bleaney's room. He stayed
The whole time he was at the Bodies, till
They moved him.' Flowered curtains, thin and frayed,
Fall to within five inches of the sill,

Whose window shows a strip of building land,
Tussocky, littered. 'Mr Bleaney took
My bit of garden properly in hand.'
Bed, upright chair, sixty-watt bulb, no hook

Behind the door, no room for books or bags –
'I'll take it.' So it happens that I lie
Where Mr Bleaney lay, and stub my fags
On the same saucer-souvenir, and try

Stuffing my ears with cotton-wool, to drown
The jabbering set he egged her on to buy.
I know his habits – what time he came down,
His preference for sauce to gravy, why

He kept on plugging at the four aways –
Likewise their yearly frame: the Frinton folk
Who put him up for summer holidays,
And Christmas at his sister's house in Stoke.

he shows what he really does through image of Mr. Bleaney.

But if he stood and watched the frigid wind
Tousling the clouds, lay on the fusty bed
Telling himself that this was home, and grinned,
And shivered, without shaking off the dread

Ends on note of non committal vagueness. Evasion - just as

That how we live measures our own nature,
And at his age having no more to show
Than one hired box should make him pretty sure
He warranted no better, I don't know.

But if he stood...
I don't know ie. whether he did or not - implying that this is what the persona does.

Nothing To Be Said

For nations vague as weed,
For nomads among stones,
Small-statured cross-faced tribes
And cobble-close families
In mill-towns on dark mornings
Life is slow dying.

So are their separate ways
Of building, benediction,
Measuring love and money
Ways of slow dying.
The day spent hunting pig
Or holding a garden-party,

Hours giving evidence
Or birth, advance
On death equally slowly.
And saying so to some
Means nothing; others it leaves
Nothing to be said.

two different types of negativity which is best - the second: awareness is all. Good example of Larkin's overall view - certain simplicity - we are born, we die, there is nothing we can do about that

Toads Revisited

Walking around in the park
Should feel better than work:
The lake, the sunshine,
The grass to lie on,

Blurred playground noises
Beyond black-stockinged nurses –
Not a bad place to be.
Yet it doesn't suit me,

Being one of the men
You meet of an afternoon:
Palsied old step-takers,
Hare-eyed clerks with the jitters,

Waxed-fleshed out-patients
Still vague from accidents,
And characters in long coats
Deep in the litter-baskets –

All dodging the toad work
By being stupid or weak.
Think of being them!
Hearing the hours chime,

Watching the bread delivered,
The sun by clouds covered,
The children going home;
Think of being them,

totally passive existence.

Turning over their failures
By some bed of lobelias,
Nowhere to go but indoors,
No friends but empty chairs –

Ironically humourous rhyme.

No, give me my in-tray,
My loaf-haired secretary,
My shall-I-keep-the-call-in-Sir:
What else can I answer,

quickening of pace. familiarity security.

104

To a certain extent within the world of work he has authority, control.

When the lights come on at four
At the end of another year?
Give me your arm, old toad;
Help me down Cemetery Road.

[handwritten: use of year as a time unit is a shock - we expect 'day'. Hints at how much time we spend at work.]

Days

What are days for?
Days are where we live.
They come, they wake us
Time and time over.
They are to be happy in:
Where can we live but days?

[handwritten: ie. we cannot live elsewhere (passivity in 3rd line) so we may as well be happy, so when we aren't happy we go mad.]

Ah, solving that question
Brings the priest and the doctor
In their long coats
Running over the fields.

[handwritten: searching for happiness]

Ambulances

Closed like confessionals, they thread
Loud noons of cities, giving back
None of the glances they absorb. *[handwritten: they take, never give.]*
Light glossy grey, arms on a plaque,
They come to rest at any kerb:
All streets in time are visited.

Then children strewn on steps or road,
Or women coming from the shops
Past smells of different dinners, see *[handwritten: hints at everyday life]*
A wild white face that overtops
Red stretcher-blankets momently
As it is carried in and stowed, *[handwritten: matter of fact, routine air]*

And sense the solving emptiness *[handwritten: 'solves' because it shows the truth - there is nothing you can do]*
That lies just under all we do,
And for a second get it whole,
So permanent and blank and true.
The fastened doors recede. *Poor soul,*
They whisper at their own distress;

For borne away in deadened air
May go the sudden shut of loss
Round something nearly at an end,   *ie patient*
And what cohered in it across   *might die*
The years, the unique random blend
Of families and fashions, there

At last begin to loosen. Far
From the exchange of love to lie
Unreachable inside a room
The traffic parts to let go by
Brings closer what is left to come,
And dulls to distance all we are.   *all means*
nothing in the end

An Arundel Tomb

Side by side, their faces blurred,
The earl and countess lie in stone,
Their proper habits vaguely shown
As jointed armour, stiffened pleat,
And that faint hint of the absurd –
The little dogs under their feet.

Such plainness of the pre-baroque
Hardly involves the eye, until
It meets his left-hand gauntlet, still
Clasped empty in the other; and
One sees, with a sharp tender shock,
His hand withdrawn, holding her hand.

They would not think to lie so long.
Such faithfulness in effigy
Was just a detail friends would see:
A sculptor's sweet commissioned grace   *ie. decision of*
Thrown off in helping to prolong   *the sculptor*
The Latin names around the base.   *that is all.*

Time
changes   They would not guess how early in
Their supine stationary voyage
The air would change to soundless damage,
Turn the old tenantry away;
How soon succeeding eyes begin
To look, not read. Rigidly they

Persisted, linked, through lengths and breadths
Of time. Snow fell, undated. Light
Each summer thronged the glass. A bright
Litter of birdcalls strewed the same
Bone-riddled ground. And up the paths
The endless altered people came,

Washing at their identity. *wearing it away*
Now, helpless in the hollow of
An unarmorial age, a trough
Of smoke in slow suspended skeins
Above their scrap of history,
Only an attitude remains:

Time has transfigured them into
Untruth. The stone fidelity
They hardly meant has come to be
Their final blazon, and to prove
Our almost-instinct almost true:
What will survive of us is love. *ie we want to believe it and here we see it is almost true - but not quite — ie it is not true at all.*

The Old Fools

What do they think has happened, the old fools,
To make them like this? Do they somehow suppose
It's more grown-up when your mouth hangs open and drools,
And you keep on pissing yourself, and can't remember
Who called this morning? Or that, if they only chose,
They could alter things back to when they danced all night,
Or went to their wedding, or sloped arms some September?
Or do they fancy there's really been no change,
And they've always behaved as if they were crippled or tight,
Or sat through days of thin continuous dreaming
Watching light move? If they don't (and they can't), it's strange:
  Why aren't they screaming? - *rejecting it.*

ie. highlighting the fact that they don't actually have any choice.

At death, you break up: the bits that were you
Start speeding away from each other for ever
With no one to see. It's only oblivion, true:
We had it before, but then it was going to end,
And was all the time merging with a unique endeavour
To bring to bloom the million-petalled flower
Of being here. Next time you can't pretend
There'll be anything else. And these are the first signs:
Not knowing how, not hearing who, the power
Of choosing gone. Their looks show that they're for it:
Ash hair, toad hands, prune face dried into lines –
      How can they ignore it?

Perhaps being old is having lighted rooms
Inside your head, and people in them, acting.
People you know, yet can't quite name; each looms
Like a deep loss restored, from known doors turning,
Setting down a lamp, smiling from a stair, extracting
A known book from the shelves; or sometimes only
The rooms themselves, chairs and a fire burning,
The blown bush at the window, or the sun's
Faint friendliness on the wall some lonely
Rain-ceased midsummer evening. That is where they live:
Not here and now, but where all happened once.
      This is why they give

An air of baffled absence, trying to be there
Yet being here. For the rooms grow farther, leaving
Incompetent cold, the constant wear and tear
Of taken breath, and them crouching below
Extinction's alp, the old fools, never perceiving
How near it is. This must be what keeps them quiet:
The peak that stays in view wherever we go
For them is rising ground. Can they never tell
What is dragging them back, and how it will end? Not at night?
Not when the strangers come? Never, throughout
The whole hideous inverted childhood? Well,
      We shall find out.

High Windows

When I see a couple of kids
And guess he's fucking her and she's
Taking pills or wearing a diaphragm,
I know this is paradise

Everyone old has dreamed of all their lives –
Bonds and gestures pushed to one side
Like an outdated combine harvester,
And everyone young going down the long slide

To happiness, endlessly. I wonder if
Anyone looked at me, forty years back,
And thought, *That'll be the life;*
No God any more, or sweating in the dark

About hell and that, or having to hide
What you think of the priest. He
And his lot will all go down the long slide
Like free bloody birds. And immediately

Rather than words comes the thought of high windows:
The sun-comprehending glass,
And beyond it, the deep blue air, that shows
Nothing, and is nowhere, and is endless.

How Distant

How distant, the departure of young men
Down valleys, or watching
The green shore past the salt-white cordage
Rising and falling,

Cattlemen, or carpenters, or keen
Simply to get away
From married villages before morning,
Melodeons play

[Handwritten annotations in margins:]

the image of the high windows represents all he has previously been saying - this is like the process of evolution is endless, evolution here rep as shedding of inhibition etc + fascinating and exhilerating but beyond it is nothing. Hints at pointlessness to this constant progression.

ironic overstatement.

As time goes on, it will always be the same.

oblivion Neither negative nor positive yet both. For this is what he wants, to rise above, yet he never will be able to.

negatives.

ie how far from him.

On tiny decks past fraying cliffs of water
Or late at night
Sweet under the differently-swung stars,
When the chance sight

Of a girl doing her laundry in the steerage
Ramifies endlessly. *branches out ie means /represents*
This is being young, *much more –*
Assumption of the startled century *like possibility*
they take it on confidently. *choice.*

hints at – Like new store clothes,
new structures/ The huge decisions printed out by feet
values. Inventing where they tread,
The random windows conjuring a street.
possibilities, beginnings.

Sad Steps

Groping back to bed after a piss
I part thick curtains, and am startled by
The rapid clouds, the moon's cleanliness.

Four o'clock: wedge-shadowed gardens lie
Under a cavernous, a wind-picked sky.
There's something laughable about this,

The way the moon dashes through clouds that blow
Loosely as cannon-smoke to stand apart
(Stone-coloured light sharpening the roofs below)

High and preposterous and separate –
Lozenge of love! Medallion of art!
O wolves of memory! Immensements! No,

One shivers slightly, looking up there.
The hardness and the brightness and the plain
Far-reaching singleness of that wide stare

Is a reminder of the strength and pain
Of being young; that it can't come again,
But is for others undiminished somewhere.

The Explosion

On the day of the explosion
Shadows pointed towards the pithead:
In the sun the slagheap slept.

Down the lane came men in pitboots
Coughing oath-edged talk and pipe-smoke,
Shouldering off the freshened silence. ie the silence in the lane they desway.

One chased after rabbits; lost them;
Came back with a nest of lark's eggs;
Showed them; lodged them in the grasses.

So they passed in beards and moleskins,
Fathers, brothers, nicknames, laughter,
Through the tall gates standing open.

At noon, there came a tremor; cows
Stopped chewing for a second; sun,
Scarfed as in a heat-haze, dimmed.

The dead go on before us, they
Are sitting in God's house in comfort,
We shall see them face to face –

Plain as lettering in the chapels
It was said, and for a second
Wives saw men of the explosion

Larger than in life they managed –
Gold as on a coin, or walking
Somehow from the sun towards them,

One showing the eggs unbroken.

NOTES

I REMEMBER, I REMEMBER

The title is an ironic allusion to Thomas Hood's poem about his idealized childhood, 'Past and Present', which opens:

> I remember, I remember
> The house where I was born,
> The little window where the sun
> Came peeping every morn.

TOADS REVISITED

A sequel to the poem 'Toads' in *The Less Deceived*. In the earlier poem, after flirting with adventure, the poet settled for his humdrum lot, realizing that he lacked the romantic courage or foolhardiness to risk shrugging off 'the toad *work*' that 'squats on my life'. In this poem he ironically celebrates the advantages of his situation as compared with that of people seen in the park.

Cemetery Road actually exists in Hull, where the poet lives; but here it lends an effective ironic-allegorical nuance.

AMBULANCES

A thread of religious imagery runs throughout the poem, serving to underline the absence of metaphysical consolation.

AN ARUNDEL TOMB

The tomb is in Chichester Cathedral. The poem may call Keats's 'Ode on a Grecian Urn' to mind, not only in the static subject with suggestively dynamic subject-matter, but also in the development of the closing stanza. Keats's final lines have the artifact witnessing to a former age and embodying in its execution values which art can perpetuate (though Keats does not commit himself to the view, defending himself with a deft use of quotation marks). Larkin shows the romantic or Keatsian view to be, in his terms, a distortion of the truth.

SAD STEPS

The title comes from Sir Philip Sidney's *Astrophel and Stella,* the sonnet beginning, 'With how sad steps, O Moon, thou climb'st the skies!', the allusion again ironic. It also recalls the poem 'Dawn' from *The North Ship,* Larkin's early collection, both in the central gesture and in the conclusion.

Elizabeth Jennings

Elizabeth Jennings was born in Boston, Lincolnshire, in 1926. While
still a child, she moved with her family to Oxford. She read English
at the University, worked as a librarian and in publishing, and
travelled in Italy. After a period of severe mental illness, she became a
freelance writer. She continues to live in Oxford. She has written
books of criticism – notably *Every Changing Shape* (1961), a critical
study of mystical and poetic expression.

A Roman Catholic by birth, her poetry has always included – in
the overtly religious verse and in the secular – the element of
sacrament. She has compared the making of poems to the exercise of
prayer: the poem attempts to reconcile the individual with what is
outside him or her, providing a momentary 'loss of self' or breach of
isolation. It is sacramental in that it binds the poet to a world of
shared particulars: words, images, rites.

Her earliest work was imitative. T. S. Eliot dictated her rhythms,
but she learned her formal principles and her prosodic art from other
masters, among them Robert Graves, W. H. Auden and Edwin
Muir. Her finest achievements are in traditionally formal verse,
though she has attempted free verse and – with success – the prose
poem. Her chief subject is relationship: between people, between
the individual and his God, and between the rational mind and
the irrational and disruptive subconscious, with its destructive
eruptions.

During the 1960s, her poems on themes suggested by her mental
illness enjoyed much popularity. It is my belief that her best work is
not from this period but from the period before and after her illness,
when the verse gained power from the successful attempt to control
the disruptive forces that were at work in her imagination. In recent
years her religious poetry has come into its own. There is a greater

technical freedom about her more recent work, a freedom exercised within traditional forms but deploying a fresh and spoken diction. Remarkable are her poems in *terza rima,* a form which has betrayed many poets before her but which she handles with great skill.

Her first collection, *Poems,* appeared in 1953. *A Way of Looking* (1955) won her the Somerset Maugham Award. Other collections include *A Sense of the World* (1958), *Song for a Birth or a Death* (1961), *Recoveries* (1964), *The Mind Has Mountains* (1966), *Collected Poems* (1967), *The Animals' Arrival* (1969), *Lucidities* (1970), *Relationships* (1972), *Growing-Points* (1975), *Consequently I Rejoice* (1977), *Moments of Grace* (1979) and *Selected Poems* (1979). She translated *The Sonnets of Michelangelo* (1961) and some poems of Arthur Rimbaud.

It is customary to associate her early work with The Movement. However, like Thom Gunn, she has little apart from her skill with traditional forms to qualify her for membership. The hallmark of The Movement is a reductive irony, and Elizabeth Jennings is no ironist or satirist, and the example of William Empson had little charm for her. She is a poet of trust and faith, not of distrust and wariness. She is more open and vulnerable as a result. There are new beginnings throughout her work, and the three best collections she has written have been composed of what one might call transitional work, a movement from one thematic procedure to another. These books are *Song for a Birth or a Death, Growing-Points,* and *Moments of Grace.*

you can't classify her.

The Island *almost a conceit.*

le longs them to it, makes them familiar to it

All travellers escape the mainland here.
The same geology torn from the stretch
Of hostile homelands is a head of calm,
And the same sea that pounds a foreign beach
Turns strangers here familiar, looses them
Kindly as pebbles shuffled up the shore.

Each brings an island in his heart to square
With what he finds, and all is something strange
But most expected. In this innocent air
Thoughts can assume a meaning, island strength
Is outward, inward, each man measures it,
Unrolls his happiness a shining length.

And this awareness grows upon itself,
Fastens on minds, is forward, backward, here.
The island focuses escape and free
Men on the shore are also islands, steer
Self to knowledge of self in the calm sea,
Seekers who are their own discovery.

[handwritten: Calm atmosphere to whole poem.]

[handwritten: island – literal and metaphorical. Where one finds oneself]

[handwritten: makes use of escape, to show us ourselves. Escapism doesn't usually mean self discovery – but that's the unusual the argument here]

[handwritten: Dissatisfaction.]

In the Night

Out of my window late at night I gape
And see the stars but do not watch them really,
And hear the trains but do not listen clearly;
Inside my mind I turn about to keep
Myself awake, yet am not there entirely.
Something of me is out in the dark landscape.

[handwritten: She stands back from herself]

How much am I then what I think, how much what I feel?
How much the eye that seems to keep stars straight?
Do I control what I can contemplate
Or is it my vision that's amenable?
I turn in my mind, my mind is a room whose wall
I can see the top of but never completely scale.

[handwritten: re controlled]

[handwritten: failure to fully know oneself]

[handwritten: objectivity]

All that I love is, like the night, outside,
Good to be gazed at, looking as if it could
With a simple gesture be brought inside my head
Or in my heart. But my thoughts about it divide
Me from my object. Now deep in my bed
I turn and the world turns on the other side.

[handwritten: She cannot fully be a part of it.]

[handwritten: Separation from it]

Ghosts

Those houses haunt in which we leave
Something undone. It is not those
Great words or silences of love

That spread their echoes through a place
And fill the locked-up unbreathed gloom.
Ghosts do not haunt with any face

That we have known; they only come
With arrogance to thrust at us
Our own omissions in a room.

The words we would not speak they use,
The deeds we dared not act they flaunt,
Our nervous silences they bruise;

It is our helplessness they choose
And our refusals that they haunt.

emphasises point that we have choice.

Choices

here speaker is apart as in 'In The Night'.
Impersonal figure offering choice.

Inside the room I see the table laid,
Four chairs, a patch of light the lamp has made

And people there so deep in tenderness
They could not speak a word of happiness.

Outside I stand and see my shadow drawn
Lengthening the clipped grass of the cared-for lawn.

Above, their roof holds half the sky behind.   *Observations*
A dog barks bringing distances to mind.

The fear of choice - the choice are could have made and now things could have been different

Comfort, I think, or safety then, or both?
I warm the cold air with my steady breath.

They have designed a way to live and I,
Clothed in confusion, set their choices by:

If so she is symptomatic of the danger + darkness ne needs the other woman?

Though sometimes one looks up and sees me there,
Alerts his shadow, pushes back his chair

ne acknowledges the other choices he had and perhaps wishes he had chosen differently - bring the darkness in

And, opening windows wide, looks out at me
And close past words we stare. It seems that he

light, cosiness - boredom.

Urges my darkness, dares it to be freed
Into that room. We need each other's need.

He needs to know that there are other possibilities

She needs to be acknowledged Need possibilities of danger/darkness in life

116

Fountain

Let it disturb no more at first
Than the hint of a pool predicted far in a forest,
Or a sea so far away that you have to open
Your window to hear it.
Think of it then as elemental, as being
Necessity,
Not for a cup to be taken to it and not   *not for human use*
For lips to linger or eye to receive itself
Back in reflection, simply
As water the patient moon persuades and stirs.   *existing for itself*

And then step closer,
Imagine rivers you might indeed embark on,
Waterfalls where you could
Silence an afternoon by staring but never
See the same tumult twice.
Yes come out of the narrow street and enter
The full piazza. Come where the noise compels.
Statues are bowing down to the breaking air.

Observe it there – the fountain, too fast for shadows,
Too wild for the lights which illuminate it to hold,
Even a moment, an ounce of water back;
Stare at such prodigality and consider
It is the elegance here, it is the taming,
The keeping fast in a thousand flowering sprays,   *psychological tension*
That builds this energy up but lets the watchers
See in that stress an image of utter calm,
A stillness there. It is how we must have felt
Once at the edge of some perpetual stream,
Fearful of touching, bringing no thirst at all,   *it don't want anything*
Panicked by no perception of ourselves   *out of it*
But drawing the water down to the deepest wonder.

as we see in her poetry –
It is an image of calm   *water seems to answer to*
but not exactly mystical   *something deeper than physical*
but certainly   *need.*
unease under the surface

117

Song for a Birth or a Death

Juxtaposition: that negativity beneath all positivity and vice versa

Balance.

Last night I saw the savage world
And heard the blood beat up the stair;
The fox's bark, the owl's shrewd pounce,
The crying creatures – all were there,
And men in bed with love and fear.

The slit moon only emphasised
How blood must flow and teeth must grip.
What does the calm light understand,
The light which draws the tide and ship
And drags the owl upon its prey
And human creatures lip to lip?

Last night I watched how pleasure must
Leap from disaster with its will:
The fox's fear, the watch-dog's lust
Know that all matings mean a kill:
And human creatures kissed in trust
Feel the blood throb to death until

The seed is struck, the pleasure's done,
The birds are thronging in the air;
The moon gives way to widespread sun.
Yes but the pain still crouches where
The young fox and the child are trapped
And cries of love are cries of fear.

My Grandmother

Life in this metaphor – unlike The Island.

She kept an antique shop – or it kept her.
Among Apostle spoons and Bristol glass,
The faded silks, the heavy furniture,
She watched her own reflection in the brass
Salvers and silver bowls, as if to prove
Polish was all, there was no need of love.

*never needed love but
& still feels guilty*

And I remember how I once refused
To go out with her, since I was afraid.
It was perhaps a wish not to be used
Like antique objects. Though she never said
That she was hurt, I still could feel the guilt
Of that refusal, guessing how she felt.

Later, too frail to keep a shop, she put
All her best things in one long narrow room.
The place smelt old, of things too long kept shut,
The smell of absences where shadows come
That can't be polished. There was nothing then
To give her own reflection back again.

Robert Frost echo

*loss of identity;
independence.*

And when she died I felt no grief at all,
Only the guilt of what I once refused.
I walked into her room among the tall
Sideboards and cupboards – things she never used
But needed: and no finger-marks were there,
Only the new dust falling through the air.

*why?
Identity,
comfort.*

She dusted it still.

death image

The Resurrection

I was the one who waited in the garden
Doubting the morning and the early light.
I watched the mist lift off its own soft burden,
Permitting not believing my own sight.

If there were sudden noises I dismissed
Them as a trick of sound, a sleight of hand.
Not by a natural joy could I be blessed
Or trust a thing I could not understand.

Maybe I was a shadow thrown by one
Who, weeping, came to lift away the stone,
Or was I but the path on which the sun,
Too heavy for itself, was loosed and thrown?

*a shadow of someone
else, the path for the
sun – re existing for
the services of some
one else.*

I heard the voices and the recognition
And love like kisses heard behind thin walls.
Were they my tears which fell, a real contrition?
Or simply April with its waterfalls?

*translating herself into
natural terms.*

It was by negatives I learnt my place.
The garden went on growing and I sensed
A sudden breeze that blew across my face.
Despair returned but now it danced, it danced.

[handwritten: Holy Spirit (greek - numa)]

[handwritten: negative + positive again]

Night Garden of the Asylum

An owl's call scrapes the stillness.
Curtains are barriers and behind them
The beds settle into neat rows. *[handwritten: Control]*
Soon they'll be ruffled.

[handwritten: images suggesting perfection - man made or not]

The garden knows nothing of illness.
Only it knows of the slow gleam
Of stars, the moon's distilling; it knows
Why the beds and lawns are levelled.

[handwritten: which beds - of the garden or the patients?]

Then all is broken from its fullness.
A human cry cuts across a dream.
A wild hand squeezes an open rose.
We are in witchcraft, bedevilled.

[handwritten: Juxtaposition of 2 images - calm of garden. Potential danger, ominous sense in the asylum]

[handwritten: why choose these images? communicates lack of understanding of situation, sense of persecution]

The Animals' Arrival *[handwritten: Creation]*

So they came
Grubbing, rooting, barking, sniffing,
Feeling for cold stars, for stone, for some hiding-place,
Loosed at last from heredity, able to eat
From any tree or from ground, merely mildly themselves,
And every movement was quick, was purposeful, was proposed.
The galaxies gazed on, drawing in their distances.
The beasts breathed out warm on the air.

[handwritten: going back to beginnings]

No-one had come to make anything of this,
To move it, name it, shape it a symbol;
The huge creatures were their own depth, the hills
Lived lofty there, wanting no climber.
Murmur of birds came, rumble of underground beasts
And the otter swam deftly over the broad river.

There was silence too.
Plants grew in it, it wove itself, it spread, it enveloped
The evening as day-calls died and the universe hushed, hushed.
A last bird flew, a first beast swam
And prey on prey
Released each other
(Nobody hunted at all):
They slept for the waiting day.

[handwritten: this is how animals are, they don't complicate things like humans. Simplicity of such a life.]

Light

To touch was an accord
Between life and life;
Later we said the word
And felt arrival of love
And enemies moving off.

A little apart we are,
(Still aware, still aware)
Light changes and shifts.
O slowly the light lifts
To show one star
And the darkness we were.

A Quartet

Four people in a street where houses were
Devoted to their silence. Voices went
Into an argument. The other pair
Looked at each other with a quiet assent.

[handwritten: facile rhyme, trying too hard?]

So speech, so echoes. What were we explaining?
Pitting ourselves against the stars perhaps?
Two did not move, or need a breath-regaining.
Pause meant a stir of love, for us a lapse

In thought. There was no feeling in our speech
Except the easing out to victory.
Tempers were kept. Better if we had each

Been silent, let the other two go off.
There was one lamp disputing with a tree.
Ideas of ours broke through those looks of love.

I Feel

I feel I could be turned to ice
If this goes on, if this goes on.
I feel I could be buried twice
And still the death not yet be done.

I feel I could be turned to fire
If there can be no end to this.
I know within me such desire
No kiss could satisfy, no kiss.

I feel I could be turned to stone,
A solid block not carved at all,
Because I feel so much alone.
I could be grave-stone or a wall.

But better to be turned to earth
Where other things at least can grow.
I could be then a part of birth,
Passive, not knowing how to know.

Rembrandt's Late Self-Portraits

You are confronted with yourself. Each year
The pouches fill, the skin is uglier.
You give it all unflinchingly. You stare
Into yourself, beyond. Your brush's care
Runs with self-knowledge. Here

Is a humility at one with craft.
There is no arrogance. Pride is apart
From this self-scrutiny. You make light drift
The way you want. Your face is bruised and hurt
But there is still love left.

Love of the art and others. To the last
Experiment went on. You stared beyond
Your age, the times. You also plucked the past
And tempered it. Self-portraits understand,
And old age can divest,

With truthful changes, us of fear of death.
Look, a new anguish. There, the bloated nose,
The sadness and the joy. To paint's to breathe,
And all the darknesses are dared. You chose
What each must reckon with.

re each darkness.

Into the Hour

I have come into the hour of a white healing.
Grief's surgery is over and I wear
The scar of my remorse and of my feeling.

I have come into a sudden sunlit hour
When ghosts are scared to corners. I have come
Into the time when grief begins to flower

Into a new love. It had filled my room
Long before I recognized it. Now
I speak its name. Grief finds its good way home.

The apple-blossom's handsome on the bough
And Paradise spreads round. I touch its grass.
I want to celebrate but don't know how.

I need not speak though everyone I pass
Stares at me kindly. I would put my hand
Into their hands. Now I have lost my loss

In some way I may later understand.
I hear the singing of the summer grass.
And love, I find, has no considered end,

Nor is it subject to the wilderness
Which follows death. I am not traitor to
A person or a memory. I trace

Behind that love another which is running
Around, ahead. I need not ask its meaning.

An Answer to Odd Advice

You who would have me often cynical
And even bitter, have you never thought
I have my moments of pure anger bought
Always highly? In my lyrical
Verse you doubtless find what you have sought,

A childishness. You should know it is hard
To keep the clear eye and the trust in men.
I have met cruelty but then, again,
I've found the good more often. I am scarred,
Like others, after unjust charges. When

You tell me to be disillusioned, I
Answer, 'I've tried and never yet succeeded
And I am glad I have not.' Hope is needed
If in a dark world some, like me, will try
To last through mankind's new Gethsemane

And be near any Christ again who's pleaded
For friends, for comfort, and not yet to die.

Goldfinch

These claws too contain
A bad crop. The goldfinch preys on the blossom
Of apple, that froth and tide of a white
Spring wedding. The neatness, the tailor-made
Touch of his suit bespeaks a harmlessness,
A wish to please that he is stranger to.

Why must we pet the world's destroyers?
I am not speaking of the soft-handed cream-buyers
Or the vendors of fresh liver
To fill the guts of a cat, no, I speak
A contradiction. I praise the pluck of the goldfinch
But I abhor this lamentable *gourmet*
Who plucks from the Eden branch the Eden flower,
Such a bright appearance, such a dandy to the inch.

Watcher

He is the watcher underneath the stars.
He dresses the dome of night with strings of long
    Meditations. He seldom moves. If he does,
It is to become acquainted with nightly creatures
    And now with hibernators who are creeping
Out of their snowy sleep, their habitations
    Which, perilously, just kept them warm enough.
The watcher is hardy and burly but even he

    Rejoices in his own silence at the change
Apparent everywhere as the glacier winter
    Slides away, as the woken grass speaks
And a chorus of thrushes and blackbirds sings the hours.
    This watcher joins them in his meditations:
But he thinks of a shadow only just beginning
    To creep over grass dressed by the sun.
It is the encroachment of a gallows-tree.
    And the watcher waits for the torment in a garden,
Eden swept out, and a dark figure weeping.

[handwritten annotations: "Nebuchadnazzar in Daniel"; "hope and despair"; "Even though spring is coming it isn't necessarily a cause for celebration."]

Thought and Feeling

[handwritten annotations: "echo of R.F. I was the one acquainted with the night"; "I have been one"; "a / a / a"; "link between stanzas"; "b / c / b / c"; "she must give that's why she gets hurt."]

I have grown wary of the ways of love
And when I find a moment crammed with thought
I cherish that sweet coolness and I move

As only spirits can, as dryads caught
In a Greek grove, then loosed among the trees.
Worship does not mean passion, I was taught.

But I have been brought down upon my knees
Was it by prayer or by the ancient church
In which I found both art and artifice?

I do not know but I know I must touch
And that it is by flesh the spirit lives.
The strides of mind are prisoned in the reach

Of sense so intricate that it receives
All impressions, sieves them as a beach
Takes worn-down, random stones and offers them

To any wanderer there on his way home.

poetry? Offering her feelings out.

On its Own

Never the same and all again.
Well, no same loss will tear me through
Or the same pain grip me if you
Go on your way. I yet shall gain
Knowledge and never wish unknown
The arguments that reach the bone,

The feelings which lay waste the heart.
No tidy place, no, I will have
All the destructiveness of love
If I can know, beyond the hurt,
Happiness waits or partly so
But not like once and long ago.

My world shall be dramatic then,
No repetitions, many acts,
A few hard treaties, broken tracts,
And peace made stronger yet by pain
Accepted but not chosen when
Love is its own and not again.

tranquillity

She will not let that real love go when she finds it.

NOTES

THE ISLAND

The oblique allusion is to Donne's *Devotions* XVII: 'No man is an Island entire of itself: every man is a piece of the Continent, a part of the main'. Also suggested is Matthew Arnold's 'To Marguerite'.

FOUNTAIN

The poet has referred back to this in a later poem as her favourite among her works.

Charles Tomlinson

Charles Tomlinson was born in Stoke-on-Trent in 1927. He was educated locally and then went to Cambridge where he was tutored by – among others – Donald Davie, with whom he shares certain qualities. Both are reluctant optimists, and Davie's Augustanism stems from the same source as Tomlinson's imagistic affinities. Both have learned important lessons from the modernists and from translation work, without forfeiting a rootedness in their particular landscapes.

Tomlinson owes a primary debt to certain American poets whose work he has helped to introduce to British readers. Wallace Stevens, Marianne Moore, William Carlos Williams and others have left a mark on him. His translations from Russian (Fyodor Tyutchev) and from Spanish (Antonio Machado, Octavio Paz and others) have further sharpened his poetic intelligence. He has a strong interest in French poetry as well.

He distrusts confessional and 'extremist' poetry and the more recent kinds of romanticism as much as Davie does. His strategy is to focus precisely on an image, an experience or an historical event, granting it its own terms, and interacting with it: the 'I' identifies itself when it intrudes so that the reader can make allowances for the inevitable distortion of subjective response. Tomlinson distrusts too great a metrical or rhythmic regularity, and his prosodic skill consists in his ability to establish a pattern and play subtle variations on it, so that the ear never relaxes but is kept attentive to each modulation of rhythm, each expressive pause. When a poem is metrically regular, the very regularity has a specific thematic point, as in the poems on French revolutionary themes. Tomlinson's characteristic stance is one of receptive wariness: he weighs each word and each perception, defining himself even as he defines the image upon which his eye focuses.

His first collection, *The Necklace* (1955), was better received in America than in Britain, and certainly his reputation until the early 1970s was higher in the United States than it was here. However, his most recent work has been widely acclaimed, and he now has a large British audience. His second collection, *Seeing is Believing* (1958, British edition 1960) was followed by *A Peopled Landscape* (1963), *American Scenes* (1966), *The Way of a World* (1969), *Written on Water* (1972), *The Way In* (1974), *The Shaft* (1978) and *Selected Poems 1951–1974* (1978). *In Black and White* (1975) was a collection of Tomlinson's accomplished graphic work, with an introduction by the Mexican poet Octavio Paz.

In his aim of 'according objects their own existence', a favourite process for Tomlinson is the return: to see an image in one light, then to come back and examine it in another. His images exist in time, in movement. Critics tend to chide Tomlinson for being 'humourless' – an unfair verdict, since he has written a number of richly amusing poems. There is also a critical case that the poems are 'poor in human interest', but the poems included here should answer such a charge. There are two related strands in Tomlinson's work: a civic strand and a more resolutely imagistic strand. Both have their source in the same quality of respect for the given, and from the poems emerges a humane aesthetic, a celebratory talent which aims at establishing balance between subject and the objective world. Tomlinson refuses to sensationalize even potentially sensational subject-matter. His poetry has the clarity of particular observation which is resonant because the poet gives it formal and temporal context.

Tramontana at Lerici

Today, should you let fall a glass it would
   Disintegrate, played off with such keenness
Against the cold's resonance (the sounds
   Hard, separate and distinct, dropping away
In a diminishing cadence) that you might swear
   This was the imitation of glass falling.

Leaf-dapples sharpen. Emboldened by this clarity
   The minds of artificers would turn prismatic,
Running on lace perforated in crisp wafers
   That could cut like steel. Constitutions,
Drafted under this fecund chill, would be annulled
   For the strictness of their equity, the moderation of their pity.

At evening, one is alarmed by such definition
  In as many lost greens as one will give glances to recover,
As many again which the landscape
  Absorbing into the steady dusk, condenses
From aquamarine to that slow indigo-pitch
  Where the light and twilight abandon themselves.

And the chill grows. In this air
  Unfit for politicians and romantics
Dark hardens from blue, effacing the windows:
  A tangible block, it will be no accessory
To that which does not concern it. One is ignored
  By so much cold suspended in so much night.

Paring the Apple

There are portraits and still-lives.

And there is paring the apple.

And then? Paring it slowly,
From under cool-yellow
Cold-white emerging. And . . .?

The spring of concentric peel
Unwinding off white,
The blade hidden, dividing.

There are portraits and still-lives
And the first, because 'human'
Does not excel the second, and
Neither is less weighted
With a human gesture, than paring the apple
With a human stillness.

The cool blade
Severs between coolness, apple-rind
Compelling a recognition.

More Foreign Cities

'Nobody wants any more poems about foreign cities. . . .'
(From a recent disquisition on poetics)

Not forgetting Ko-jen, that
Musical city (it has
Few buildings and annexes
Space by combating silence),
There is Fiordiligi, its sun-changes
Against walls of transparent stone
Unsettling all preconception – a city
For architects (they are taught
By casting their nets
Into those moving shoals); and there is
Kairouan, whose lit space
So slides into and fits
The stone masses, one would doubt
Which was the more solid
Unless, folding back
Gold segments out of the white
Pith globe of a quartered orange,
One may learn perhaps
To read such perspectives. At Luna
There is a city of bridges, where
Even the inhabitants are mindful
Of a shared privilege: a bridge
Does not exist for its own sake.
It commands vacancy.

At Holwell Farm

It is a quality of air, a temperate sharpness
   Causes an autumn fire to burn compact,
To cast from a shapely and unrifted core
   Its steady brightness. A kindred flame
Gathers within the stone, and such a season
   Fosters, then frees it in a single glow:

Pears by the wall and stone as ripe as pears
    Under the shell-hood's cornice; the door's
Bright oak, the windows' slim-cut frames
    Are of an equal whiteness. Crude stone
By a canopy of shell, each complements
    In opposition, each is bound
Into a pattern of utilities – this farm
    Also a house, this house a dwelling.
Rooted in more than earth, to dwell
    Is to discern the Eden image, to grasp
In a given place and guard it well
    Shielded in stone. Whether piety
Be natural, is neither the poet's
    Nor the builder's story, but a quality of air,
Such as surrounds and shapes an autumn fire
    Bringing these sharp disparities to bear.

The Picture of J. T.
in a Prospect of Stone

What should one
        wish a child
                and that, one's own
    emerging
            from between
                    the stone lips
    of a sheep-stile
            that divides
                    village graves
    and village green?
            – Wish her
                    the constancy of stone.
    – But stone
            is hard.
                    – Say, rather
    it resists
            the slow corrosives
                    and the flight
    of time
            and yet it takes
                    the play, the fluency
    from light.

131

          – How would you know
             the gift you'd give
was the gift
      she'd wish to have?
         – Gift is giving,
gift is meaning:
      first
          I'd give
then let her
      live with it
          to prove
its quality the better and
      thus learn
          to love
what (to begin with)
      she might spurn.
         – You'd
moralize a gift?
      – I'd have her
          understand
the gift I gave her.
        – And so she shall
          but let her play
her innocence away
      emerging
          as she does
between
      her doom (unknown),
          her unmown green.

The Snow Fences

They are fencing the upland against
the drifts this wind, those clouds
would bury it under: brow and bone
know already that levelling zero
as you go, an aching skeleton,
in the breathtaking rareness of winter air.

Walking here, what do you see?
Little more, through wind-teased eyes,
than a black, iron tree

and, there, another, a straggle
of low and broken wall between, grass
sapped of its greenness, day going.

The farms are few: spread
as wide, perhaps, as when
the Saxons who found them, chose
these airy and woodless spaces
and froze here before they fed
the unsuperseded burial ground.

Ahead, the church's dead-white
limewash will dazzle the mind
as, dazed, you enter to escape:
despite the stillness here, the chill
of wash-light scarcely seems
less penetrant than the hill-top wind.

Between the graves, you find
a beheaded pigeon, the blood and grain
trailed from its bitten crop, as alien to all
the day's pallor as the raw
wounds of the earth, turned above
a fresh solitary burial.

A plaque of staining metal
distinguishes this grave among
an anonymity whose stones
the frosts have scaled, thrusting under
as if they grudged the ground
its ill-kept memorials.

The bitter darkness drives you
back valleywards, and again you bend
joint and tendon to encounter
the wind's force and leave behind
the nameless stones, the snow-shrouds
of a waste season: they are fencing
the upland against those years, those clouds.

Swimming Chenango Lake

Winter will bar the swimmer soon.
   He reads the water's autumnal hesitations
A wealth of ways: it is jarred,
   It is astir already despite its steadiness,
Where the first leaves at the first
   Tremor of the morning air have dropped
Anticipating him, launching their imprints
   Outwards in eccentric, overlapping circles.
There is a geometry of water, for this
   Squares off the clouds' redundances
And sets them floating in a nether atmosphere
   All angles and elongations: every tree
Appears a cypress as it stretches there
   And every bush that shows the season,
A shaft of fire. It is a geometry and not
   A fantasia of distorting forms, but each
Liquid variation answerable to the theme
   It makes away from, plays before:
It is a consistency, the grain of the pulsating flow.
   But he has looked long enough, and now
Body must recall the eye to its dependence
   As he scissors the waterscape apart
And sways it to tatters. Its coldness
   Holding him to itself, he grants the grasp,
For to swim is also to take hold
   On water's meaning, to move in its embrace
And to be, between grasp and grasping, free.
   He reaches in-and-through to that space
The body is heir to, making a where
   In water, a possession to be relinquished
Willingly at each stroke. The image he has torn
   Flows-to behind him, healing itself,
Lifting and lengthening, splayed like the feathers
   Down an immense wing whose darkening spread
Shadows his solitariness: alone, he is unnamed
   By this baptism, where only Chenango bears a name
In a lost language he begins to construe –
   A speech of densities and derisions, of half-
Replies to the questions his body must frame

Frogwise across the all but penetrable element.
Human, he fronts it and, human, he draws back
    From the interior cold, the mercilessness
That yet shows a kind of mercy sustaining him.
    The last sun of the year is drying his skin
Above a surface a mere mosaic of tiny shatterings,
    Where a wind is unscaping all images in the flowing obsidian,
The going-elsewhere of ripples incessantly shaping.

Prometheus

Summer thunder darkens, and its climbing
    Cumulae, disowning our scale in the zenith,
Electrify this music: the evening is falling apart.
    Castles-in-air; on earth: green, livid fire.
The radio simmers with static to the strains
    Of this mock last-day of nature and of art.

We have lived through apocalypse too long:
    Scriabin's dinosaurs! Trombones for the transformation
That arrived by train at the Finland Station,
    To bury its hatchet after thirty years in the brain
Of Trotsky. Alexander Nikolayevitch, the events
    Were less merciful than your mob of instruments.

Too many drowning voices cram this waveband.
    I set Lenin's face by yours –
Yours, the fanatic ego of eccentricity against
    The systematic son of a schools inspector
Tyutchev on desk – for the strong man reads
    Poems as the antisemite pleads: 'A Jew was my friend.'

Cymballed firesweeps. Prometheus came down
    In more than orchestral flame and Kérensky fled
Before it. The babel of continents gnaws now
    And tears at the silk of those harmonies that seemed
So dangerous once. You dreamed an end
    Where the rose of the world would go out like a close
                                        in music.

Population drags the partitions down
   And we are a single town of warring suburbs:
I cannot hear such music for its consequence:
   Each sense was to have been reborn
Out of a storm of perfumes and light
   To a white world, an in-the-beginning.

In the beginning, the strong man reigns:
   Trotsky, was it not then you brought yourself
To judgement and to execution, when you forgot
   Where terror rules, justice turns arbitrary?
Chromatic Prometheus, myth of fire,
   It is history topples you in the zenith.

Blok, too, wrote The Scythians
   Who should have known: he who howls
With the whirlwind, with the whirlwind goes down.
   In this, was Lenin guiltier than you
When, out of a merciless patience grew
   The daily prose such poetry prepares for?

Scriabin, Blok, men of extremes,
   History treads out the music of your dreams
Through blood, and cannot close like this
   In the perfection of anabasis. It stops. The trees
Continue raining though the rain has ceased
   In a cooled world of incessant codas:

Hard edges of the houses press
   On the after-music senses, and refuse to burn,
Where an ice-cream van circulates the estate
   Playing Greensleeves, and at the city's
Stale new frontier even ugliness
   Rules with the cruel mercy of solidities.

Against Extremity

Let there be treaties, bridges,
   Chords under the hands, to be spanned
Sustained: extremity hates a given good

Or a good gained. That girl who took
Her life almost, then wrote a book
   To exorcise and to exhibit the sin,
Praises a friend there for the end she made
   And each of them becomes a heroine.
The time is in love with endings. The time's
   Spoiled children threaten what they will do,
And those they cannot shake by petulance
   They'll bribe out of their wits by show.
Against extremity, let there be
   Such treaties as only time itself
Can ratify, a bond and test
   Of sequential days, and like the full
Moon slowly given to the night,
   A possession that is not to be possessed.

The Fox Gallery

A long house –
the fox gallery you called
its upper storey, because
you could look down to see
(and did) the way a fox would
cross the field beyond
and you could follow out, window
to window, the fox's way
the whole length of the meadow
parallel with the restraining line
of wall and pane, or as far
as that could follow the sense of all
those windings. Do you remember
the morning I woke you with the cry
Fox fox and the animal
came on – not from side
to side, but straight
at the house and we craned
to see more and more, the most
we could of it and then
watched it sheer off deterred
by habitation, and saw
how utterly the two worlds were

disparate, as that perfect
ideogram for agility
and liquefaction flowed
away from us rhythmical
and flickering and
that flare was final.

Of Beginning Light

The light of the mind is poorer
than beginning light: the shades
we find pigment for
poor beside the tacit
variety we can all see
yet cannot say: of beginning light
I will say this, that it dispenses
imperial equality to everything
it touches, so that purple
becomes common wear, but purple
resolving in its chord
a thousand tones
tinged by a thousand
shadows, all
yielding themselves
slowly up: and the mind,
feeling its way among
such hesitant distinctions,
is left behind as they
flare into certainties that
begin by ending them
in the light of day.

In Memoriam Thomas Hardy

How to speak with the dead
so that not only
our but their
words are valid?

Unlike their stones,
they scarcely resist us,
memory adjusting
its shades, its mist:

they are too like their photographs
where we can fill
with echoes of our regrets
brown worlds of stillness.

His besetting word
was 'afterwards' and it released
their qualities, their restlessness
as though they heard it.

The Marl Pits

It was a language of water, light and air
    I sought – to speak myself free of a world
Whose stoic lethargy seemed the one reply
    To horizons and to streets that blocked them back
In a monotone fume, a bloom of grey.
    I found my speech. The years return me
To tell of all that seasoned and imprisoned:
    I breathe familiar, sedimented air
From a landscape of disembowellings, underworlds
    Unearthed among the clay. Digging
The marl, they dug a second nature
    And water, seeping up to fill their pits,
Sheeted them to lakes that wink and shine
    Between tips and steeples, streets and waste
In slow reclaimings, shimmers, balancings,
    As if kindling Eden rescinded its own loss
And words and water came of the same source.

After a Death

A little ash, a painted rose, a name.
    A moonshell that the blinding sky

Puts out with winter blue, hangs
  Fragile at the edge of visibility. That space
Drawing the eye up to its sudden frontier
  Asks for a sense to read the whole
Reverted side of things. I wanted
  That height and prospect such as music brings –
Music or memory. Neither brought me here.
  This burial place straddles a green hill,
Chimneys and steeples plot the distances
  Spread vague below: only the sky
In its upper reaches keeps
  An untarnished January colour. Verse
Fronting that blaze, that blade,
  Turns to retrace the path of its dissatisfactions,
Thought coiled on thought, and only certain that
  Whatever can make bearable or bridge
The waste of air, a poem cannot.
  The husk of moon, risking the whole of space,
Seemingly sails it, frailly launched
  To its own death and fulness. We buried
A little ash. Time so broke you down,
  Your lost eyes, dry beneath
Their matted lashes, a painted rose
  Seems both to memorialize and mock
What you became. It picks your name out
  Written on the roll beside a verse –
Obstinate words: measured against the blue,
  They cannot conjure with the dead. Words,
Bringing that space to bear, that air
  Into each syllable we speak, bringing
An earnest to us of the portion
  We must inherit, what thought of that would give
The greater share of comfort, greater fear –
  To live forever, or to cease to live?
The imageless unnaming upper blue
  Defines a world, all images
Of endeavours uncompleted. Torn levels
  Of the land drop, street by street,
Pitted and pooled, its wounds
  Cleansed by a light, dealt out
With such impartiality you'd call it kindness,
  Blindly assuaging where assuagement goes unfelt.

For Danton

'Bound to the fierce Metropolis . . .'
THE PRELUDE, BOOK X

In the autumn of 1793 – the year in which he had instituted the
Revolutionary Tribunal – Danton went back to his birthplace,
Arcis-sur-Aube. After his return in November, he was to be arrested,
tried and condemned.

Who is the man that stands against this bridge
And thinks that he and not the river advances?
Can he not hear the links of consequence
Chiming his life away? Water is time.
Not yet, not yet. He fronts the parapet
Drinking the present with unguarded sense:

The stream comes on. Its music deafens him
To other sounds, to past and future wrong.
The beat is regular beneath that song.
He hears in it a pulse that is his own;
He hears the year autumnal and complete.
November waits for him who has not done

With seeings, savourings. Grape-harvest brings
The south into the north. This parapet
Carries him forward still, a ship from Rheims,
From where, in boyhood and on foot, he'd gone
'To see,' he said, 'the way a king is made',
The king that he himself was to uncrown –

Destroyed and superseded, then secure
In the possession of a perfect power
Returned to this: to river, town and plain,
Walked in the fields and knew what power he'd lost,
The cost to him of that metropolis where
He must come back to rule and Robespierre.

Not yet. This contrary perfection he
Must taste into a life he has no time
To live, a lingered, snatched maturity
Before he catches in the waterchime
The measure and the chain a death began,
And fate that loves the symmetry of rhyme
Will spring the trap whose teeth must have a man.

In Arden

'This is the forest of Arden . . .'

Arden is not Eden, but Eden's rhyme:
   Time spent in Arden is time at risk
And place, also: for Arden lies under threat:
   Ownership will get what it can for Arden's trees:
No acreage of green-belt complacencies
   Can keep Macadam out: Eden lies guarded:
Pardonable Adam, denied its gate,
   Walks the grass in a less-than-Eden light
And whiteness that shines from a stone burns with his fate:
   Sun is tautening the field's edge shadowline
Along the wood beyond: but the contraries
   Of this place are contrarily unclear:
A haze beats back the summer sheen
   Into a chiaroscuro of the heat:
The down on the seeded grass that beards
   Each rise where it meets with sky,
Ripples a gentle fume: a fine
   Incense, smelling of hay smokes by:
Adam in Arden tastes its replenishings:
   Through its dense heats the depths of Arden's springs
Convey echoic waters – voices
   Of the place that rises through this place,
Overflowing, as it brims its surfaces
   In runes and hidden rhymes, in chords and keys
Where Adam, Eden, Arden run together
   And time itself must beat to the cadence of this river.

NOTES

TRAMONTANA AT LERICI

Tramontana: north wind.

Lerici: in Liguria, Italy, where Shelley spent his last months before he was drowned. One recalls – given the imagery – Shelley's lines from *Adonaïs*, his elegy for Keats: 'Time like a dome of many-coloured glass/Stains the white radiance of eternity'.

MORE FOREIGN CITIES

The epigraph was uttered by Kingsley Amis. The four cities (or towns) chosen – Japanese, Italian, Tunisian and New Mexican – are in themselves, without the addition of argument, a sufficient refutation. They indicate what Amis's prescriptive and reductive aesthetic would exclude.

THE PICTURE OF J.T. IN A PROSPECT OF STONE

J.T.: the poet's daughter. The title is meant to recall Andrew Marvell's 'Picture of Little T. C. in a Prospect of Flowers'. The poem is related generically to those of Coleridge and Yeats on the same subject, and in its opening lines recalls Edward Thomas's poems to his children. Tomlinson here exploits a quiet dialogue form.

SWIMMING CHENANGO LAKE

Chenango: the Indian name of a lake and park in New York State.

PROMETHEUS

The title refers not only to the mythical figure – so loved of the romantics – who brought man fire from heaven and was cruelly punished by the gods. It is also a specific allusion to the Russian composer *Alexander Nikolayevitch Scriabin's* tone poem 'Prometheus', a revolutionary piece of music that tries to combine various media. In Tomlinson's poem, the music heard on the radio is accompanied by a literal storm which adds an aural, visual and symbolic dimension. The revolutionary Russian music takes the poet's mind to the Russian Revolution itself and its attempt to impose a millennial ideology on an intractable human and social reality. The poem traces the process by which abstract and philosophical ideas, applied to life, are literalized and transformed from their intent into cruel systems. The poet alludes to the arrival of the Bolsheviks at the Finland Station, to the eventual 'hatchet' murder in Mexico of *Leon Trotsky* (subject of Tomlinson's poem 'Assassin'), to the romantic poet *Fyodor Tyutchev* (1803–73) whom Tomlinson translated, to the liberal leader *Kérensky* whom the Bolsheviks ousted, and to the poet *Alexander Blok* (1880–1921) who wrote 'The Scythians' in his early enthusiasm for the Revolution but who shortly thereafter fell silent. Of Blok, Trotsky wrote, 'Certainly he was not one of us, but he came towards us. And that broke him.' 'Prometheus' is Tomlinson's strongest indictment of the distortions of ideology and romanticism and of the complicity of the irresponsible artist in the events for which his art provides a context or a pretext. Though the history evoked is specifically Russian, the poem has explicit implications for non-Marxist totalitarian ideologies as well.

AGAINST EXTREMITY

Originally this poem bore the dedication, 'In Memoriam A. A.', a reference to Al Alvarez, editor of *The New Poetry,* an assiduous promoter of the 'extremity' Tomlinson is so strongly opposed to.

That girl: Anne Sexton (1928–76), the American poet, whose poem 'Sylvia's Death' (about Sylvia Plath) epitomized for Tomlinson the absurdity of a bankrupt and bankrupting extremist aesthetic.

AFTER A DEATH

This elegy for Tomlinson's mother returns to the place of his birth and her death, Stoke-on-Trent. His past is clarified here by a controlled grief. The poem is from 'Under the Moon's Reign' which forms part two of the sequence 'The Way In'.

FOR DANTON

Georges Danton (1759–94) – lawyer and administrator – led the right wing of the Jacobins in the French Revolution and was instrumental in felling the monarchy.

The epigraph, from Wordsworth's *Prelude,* Book X, has this context:

> Green meadow-ground, and many-coloured woods
> Again and yet again, a farewell look;
> Then from the quiet of that scene passed on,
> Bound to the fierce metropolis . . .

Maximilian de Robespierre (1758–94) eventually had Danton arraigned before the Revolutionary Tribunal and executed with his followers (6 April, 1794). Robespierre himself, instigator of the Reign of Terror, followed Danton to the guillotine later in the year.

IN ARDEN

The title is from Shakespeare's *As You Like It* (III, iv, l. 14):

> *Rosalind*: Well, this is the Forest of Arden.
> *Touchstone* (the Fool): Ay now am I in Arden, the more fool I. When I was at home, I was in a better place, but travellers must be content.

The Arden/Eden, real/ideal tension runs through Tomlinson's work. Echo and reflection in Arden suggest the Eden world.

Thom Gunn

Thom Gunn was born in 1929 at Gravesend. He studied at Cambridge where, while still an undergraduate, he published a pamphlet collection with The Fantasy Press. This was *Fighting Terms* (1954), the work of a young man of extraordinary verbal dexterity and of what one might call a *timely* intelligence. The poet was in touch not only with English literature but with certain threads of European thought, notably with the writings of Sartre. His subject-matter recommended him to his own and the following generation, while his formal skills won the approval of the older generation. Late in 1954 he went to Stanford University in California as a student and teacher. There he had the advantage of the teaching of Yvor Winters (see 'To Yvor Winters, 1955', p. 150). Gunn has travelled widely (on his Somerset Maugham Award he visited Italy), but he has made his home in California, and his thematic and linguistic developments as a poet have inevitably been much affected by his experiences there.

In the 1950s his work came misleadingly to be associated with The Movement (see p. 5). He was neither an ironist in the spirit of Amis, however, nor a bleak realist in the spirit of Larkin. His craving for large meanings and his growing desire to present experience in a personal and straightforward fashion led him, in a spirit of quest, from the early poems in traditional accentual-syllabic form to rhymed syllabic verse and to free verse. He has recognized how different experiences and occasions require different forms: an epigrammatic poem must rhyme, while a poem lacking the finality of epigram and which is of its nature tentative will work best in free verse. His English roots are deep in the sixteenth and seventeenth centuries: Fulke Greville, George Gascoigne, Ben Jonson and the Jacobean dramatists (among others) provided early bearings. Yvor Winters and Elizabeth Daryush (rather than Marianne Moore) suggested his distinctive syllabic disciplines. The logic underlying his free verse owes much to D. H. Lawrence and, in terms of organization, to Ezra Pound.

He writes in order to move forward. The verse has strong personal themes and, especially in the earliest work, the reader tends to look at the poet, rather than through him at the experience. Even in his free verse Gunn is immensely self-conscious, a performer in the plot some of the time, always a conscious virtuoso in his prosody. Yet from an almost allegorical form of early presentation he has moved through a more symbolic to an almost imagistic idiom at times – still ruthlessly deliberate, but occasionally allowing himself to cross a deep chasm on a flimsy board of words. When he takes such risks he can at times reach his finest effects. Critics have tended to see his later work as 'a falling off'. It is, in fact, a change, a series of new beginnings. Tired of the efficiency of his early style, he has apparently decided that the best way to advance is the risky way of leaving the predictable path, armed still with his great skills, and exploring the terrain that challenges him either side of certainty.

After *Fighting Terms*, his collections are *The Sense Of Movement* (1957), *My Sad Captains* (1961), *Touch* (1967), *Positives* (1966, 1973), *Moly* (1971) and *Jack Straw's Castle* (1976). Selections – *Poems 1950–1966* and *Selected Poems by Thom Gunn and Ted Hughes* – have also been published. His prose essays are illuminating – in particular his introduction to the *Selected Poems* of Ben Jonson (Penguin, 1974).

A Mirror for Poets

It was a violent time. Wheels, racks, and fires
In every writer's mouth, and not mere rant.
Certain shrewd herdsmen, between twisted wires
Of penalty folding the realm, were thanked
For organizing spies and secret police
By richness in the flock, which they could fleece.

Hacks in the Fleet and nobles in the Tower:
Shakespeare must keep the peace, and Jonson's thumb
Be branded (for manslaughter), to the power
Of irons the admired Southampton's power was come.
Above all swayed the diseased and doubtful queen:
Her state canopied by the glamour of pain.

In this society the boundaries met
Of life and life, at danger; with no space
Being left between, except where might be set
That mathematical point whose time and place
Could not exist. Yet at this point they found
Arcadia, a fruitful permanent land.

The faint and stumbling crowds were dim to sight
Who had no time for pity or for terror:
Here moved the Forms, flooding like moonlight,
In which the act or thought perceived its error.
The hustling details, calmed and relevant.
Here mankind might behold its whole extent.

Here in a cave the Paphlagonian King
Crouched, waiting for his greater counterpart
Who one remove from likelihood may seem,
But several nearer to the human heart.
In exile from dimension, change by storm,
Here his huge magnanimity was born.

Yet the historians tell us, life meant less.
It was a violent time, and evil-smelling.
Jonson howled 'Hell's a grammar-school to this,'
But found renunciation well worth telling.
Winnowing with his flail of comedy *neat*
He showed coherence in society.

In street, in tavern, happening would cry
'I am myself, but part of something greater,
Find poets what that is, do not pass by,
For feel my fingers in your pia mater.
I am a cruelly insistent friend:
You cannot smile at me and make an end.'

On The Move *difficult to para-phrase, even though it seems to be explaining itself*

'Man, you gotta Go.'

The blue jay scuffling in the bushes follows
Some hidden purpose, and the gust of birds
That spurts across the field, the wheeling swallows,

Choosing to be what you are 148 *} extremes of existentialism*
having no control over what you are

Have nested in the trees and undergrowth.
Seeking their instinct, or their poise, or both,
One moves with an uncertain violence
Under the dust thrown by a baffled sense
Or the dull thunder of approximate words.

the motorcyclists embody these abstract images.

On motorcycles, up the road, they come:
Small, black, as flies hanging in heat, the Boys,
Until the distance throws them forth, their hum
Bulges to thunder held by calf and thigh.
In goggles, donned impersonality,
In gleaming jackets trophied with the dust,
They strap in doubt – by hiding it, robust –
And almost hear a meaning in their noise.

funny
they too move with uncertain violence
these are their words.

Exact conclusion of their hardiness
Has no shape yet, but from known whereabouts
They ride, direction where the tires press.
They scare a flight of birds across the field:
Much that is natural, to the will must yield.
Men manufacture both machine and soul,
And use what they imperfectly control
To dare a future from the taken routes.

It is a part solution, after all.
One is not necessarily discord
On earth; or damned because, half animal,
One lacks direct instinct, because one wakes
Afloat on movement that divides and breaks.
One joins the movement in a valueless world,
Choosing it, till, both hurler and the hurled,
One moves as well, always toward, toward.

✻ Contemplation of the human significance of their kind of action.

Sum up paradox of phrases
He can't sum up experience in this way became dissatisfied with way he wrote.

A minute holds them, who have come to go:
The self-defined, astride the created will
They burst away; the towns they travel through
Are home for neither bird nor holiness,
For birds and saints complete their purposes.
At worst, one is in motion; and at best,
Reaching no absolute, in which to rest,
One is always nearer by not keeping still.

the way we live life – life is so full of activities etc. but how much of it means anything? How much do we pack in to keep at bay our fears?

California

149

To Yvor Winters, 1955

I leave you in your garden.
                In the yard
Behind it, run the airedales you have reared
With boxer's vigilance and poet's rigour:
Dog-generations you have trained the vigour
That few can breed to train and fewer still
Control with the deliberate human will.
And in the house there rest, piled shelf on shelf,
The accumulations that compose the self –
Poem and history: for if we use
Words to maintain the actions that we choose,
Our words, with slow defining influence,
Stay to mark out our chosen lineaments.

Continual temptation waits on each
To renounce his empire over thought and speech,
Till he submit his passive faculties
To evening, come where no resistance is;
The unmotivated sadness of the air
Filling the human with his own despair.
Where now lies power to hold the evening back?
Implicit in the grey is total black:
Denial of the discriminating brain
Brings the neurotic vision, and the vein
Of necromancy. All as relative
For mind as for the sense, we have to live
In a half-world, not ours nor history's,
And learn the false from half-true premises.

But sitting in the dusk – though shapes combine,
Vague mass replacing edge and flickering line,
You keep both Rule and Energy in view,
Much power in each, most in the balanced two:
Ferocity existing in the fence
Built by an exercised intelligence.
Though night is always close, complete negation
Ready to drop on wisdom and emotion,
Night from the air or the carnivorous breath,
Still it is right to know the force of death,

150

Handwritten marginal annotations:

- suggests his strength
- What?
- re this would be the result if we abandoned *
- witchcraft we must delineate things have them purely communicated in words
- re not in our history's world where in hindsight we see all, not just half
- Ferocity/passion present but reigned in, fenced, controlled. This is where power is
- Balance

And, as you do, persistent, tough in will,
Raise from the excellent the better still.

In Santa Maria del Popolo

Waiting for when the sun an hour or less
Conveniently oblique makes visible
The painting on one wall of this recess
By Caravaggio, of the Roman School,
I see how shadow in the painting brims
With a real shadow, drowning all shapes out
But a dim horse's haunch and various limbs,
Until the very subject is in doubt.

But evening gives the act, beneath the horse
And one indifferent groom, I see him sprawl,
Foreshortened from the head, with hidden face,
Where he has fallen, Saul becoming Paul.
O wily painter, limiting the scene
From a cacophony of dusty forms
To the one convulsion, what is it you mean
In that wide gesture of the lifting arms?

No Ananias croons a mystery yet,
Casting the pain out under name of sin.
The painter saw what was, an alternate
Candour and secrecy inside the skin.
He painted, elsewhere, that firm insolent
Young whore in Venus' clothes, those pudgy cheats,
Those sharpers; and was strangled, as things went,
For money, by one such picked off the streets.

I turn, hardly enlightened, from the chapel
To the dim interior of the church instead,
In which there kneel already several people,
Mostly old women: each head closeted
In tiny fists holds comfort as it can.
Their poor arms are too tired for more than this
– For the large gesture of solitary man,
Resisting, by embracing, nothingness.

151

an ordinary person.

Innocence

form of ignorance.

(to Tony White)

He ran the course and as he ran he grew,
And smelt his fragrance in the field. Already,
Running he knew the most he ever knew,
The egotism of a healthy body.

as opposed to Anton Smidt.

Ran into manhood, ignorant of the past:
Culture of guilt and guilt's vague heritage,
Self-pity and the soul; what he possessed
Was rich, potential, like the bud's tipped rage.

The Corps developed, it was plain to see,
Courage, endurance, loyalty and skill

keep people together as a Corps

To a morale firm as morality, *but it isn't morality*
Hardening him to an instrument, until

The finitude of virtues that were there
Bodied within the swarthy uniform
A compact innocence, child-like and clear,
No doubt could penetrate, no act could harm.

When he stood near the Russian partisan
Being burned alive, he therefore could behold
The ribs wear gently through the darkening skin
And sicken only at the Northern cold,

Michael Schmidt – amoral integrity – integrity meaning wholeness.

Could watch the fat burn with a violet flame
And feel disgusted only at the smell,
And judge that all pain finishes the same
As melting quietly by his boots it fell.

Links with Epitaph for Anton Schmidt, who is to be approved.

Considering the Snail

The snail pushes through a green
night, for the grass is heavy

with water and meets over
the bright path he makes, where rain
has darkened the earth's dark. He
moves in a wood of desire,

pale antlers barely stirring
as he hunts. I cannot tell
what power is at work, drenched there
with purpose, knowing nothing.
What is a snail's fury? All
I think is that if later

I parted the blades above
the tunnel and saw the thin
trail of broken white across
litter, I would never have
imagined the slow passion
to that deliberate progress.

My Sad Captains

One by one they appear in
the darkness: a few friends, and
a few with historical
names. How late they start to shine!
but before they fade they stand
perfectly embodied, all

the past lapping them like a
cloak of chaos. They were men
who, I thought, lived only to
renew the wasteful force they
spent with each hot convulsion.
They remind me, distant now.

True, they are not at rest yet,
but now that they are indeed
apart, winnowed from failures,
they withdraw to an orbit
and turn with disinterested
hard energy, like the stars.

held in a moment
of time, before
defeat.

153

Touch

You are already
asleep. I lower
myself in next to
you, my skin slightly
numb with the restraint
of habits, the patina of
self, the black frost
of outsideness, so that even
unclothed it is
a resilient chilly
hardness, a superficially
malleable, dead
rubbery texture.

You are a mound
of bedclothes, where the cat
in sleep braces
its paws against your
calf through the blankets,
and kneads each paw in turn.

Meanwhile and slowly
I feel a is it *hesitation*
my own warmth surfacing or
the ferment of your whole
body that in darkness beneath
the cover is stealing
bit by bit to break
down that chill.

            You turn and
hold me tightly, do
you know who
I am or am I *mirror image*
your mother or
the nearest human being to
hold on to in a
dreamed pogrom. *massacre (Jewish)*
victimisation

What I, now loosened,
sink into is an old
big place, it is
there already, for
you are already
there, and the cat
got there before you, yet
it is hard to locate.
What is more, the place is
not found but seeps
from our touch in
continuous creation, dark
enclosing cocoon round
ourselves alone, dark   *In sleep we are alone*
wide realm where we   *yet can be with*
walk with everyone. . .   *people*

Epitaph for Anton Schmidt

The Schmidts obeyed, and marched on Poland.
And there an Anton Schmidt, Feldwebel, *seargent.*
Performed uncommon things, not safe,
Nor glamorous, nor profitable.

Was the expression on his face
'Reposeful and humane good nature'?
Or did he look like any Schmidt,
Of slow and undisclosing feature?

I know he had unusual eyes,
Whose power no orders might determine,
Not to mistake the men he saw,
As others did, for gods or vermin.
                  germans   Jews
For five months, till his execution,
Aware that action has its dangers,
He helped the Jews to get away
– Another race at that, and strangers.

155

He never did mistake for bondage
The military job, the chances,
The limits; he did not submit
To the blackmail of his circumstances.

ie If marching on Poland must be on Hitler's side but he decided to help the Jews

I see him in the Polish snow,
His muddy wrappings small protection,
Breathing the cold air of his freedom
And treading a distinct direction.
his own

Rites of Passage

Something is taking place.
Horns bud bright in my hair.
My feet are turning hoof.
And Father, see my face
– Skin that was damp and fair
Is barklike and, feel, rough.

See Greytop how I shine.
I rear, break loose, I neigh
Snuffing the air, and harden
Towards a completion, mine.
And next I make my way
Adventuring through your garden.

My play is earnest now.
I canter to and fro.
My blood, it is like light.
Behind an almond bough,
Horns gaudy with its snow,
I wait live, out of sight.

All planned before my birth
For you, Old Man, no other,
Whom your groin's trembling warns.
I stamp upon the earth
A message to my mother.
And then I lower my horns.

156

THOM GUNN

The Garden of the Gods

All plants grow here; the most minute,
  Glowing from turf, is in its place.
  The constant vision of the race:
Lawned orchard deep with flower and fruit.

So bright, that some who see it near,
  Think there is lapis on the stems,
  And think green, blue, and crimson gems
Hang from the vines and briars here.

They follow path to path in wonder
  Through the intense undazzling light.
  Nowhere does blossom flare so white!
Nowhere so black is earthmould under!

It goes, though it may come again.
  But if at last they try to tell,
  They search for trope or parallel,   *figurative use of word ie metaphor*
And cannot, after all, explain.

It was sufficient, there, to be,
  And meaning, thus, was superseded.
  – Night circles it, it has receded,
Distant and difficult to see.

Where my foot rests, I hear the creak
  From generations of my kin,
  Layer on layer, pressed leaf-thin.
They merely are. They cannot speak.

This was the garden's place of birth: *– In his past, his family?*
  I trace it downward from my mind,
  Through breast and calf I feel it vined,
And rooted in the death-rich earth.

    It is in himself?

A sense of place/ belonging
Poetic inspiration

157

Diagrams

Downtown, an office tower is going up.
And from the mesa of unfinished top   *U.S A Isolated flat top*
Big cranes jut, spectral points of stiffened net: *hill*
Angled top-heavy artefacts, and yet
Diagrams from the sky, as if its air
Could drop lines, snip them off, and leave them there.

makes a building into something else

On girders round them, Indians pad like cats,
With wrenches in their pockets and hard hats.

They wear their yellow boots like moccasins,
Balanced where air ends and where steel begins,
Sky men, and through the sole's flesh, chewed and pliant,
They feel the studded bone-edge of the giant.
It grunts and sways through its whole metal length.
And giving to the air is sign of strength.

*bigness, newness he has admiration for.
Going into new areas.*

Iron Landscapes
(and the Statue of Liberty)

No trellisses, no vines
                    a fire escape
Repeats a bare black Z from tier to tier.
Hard flower, tin scroll embellish this landscape.
Between iron columns I walk toward the pier.

And stand a long time at the end of it
Gazing at iron on the New Jersey side.
A girdered ferry-building opposite,
Displaying the name LACKAWANNA, seems to ride

The turbulent brown-grey waters that intervene:
Cool seething incompletion that I love.
The zigzags come and go, sheen tracking sheen;
And water wrestles with the air above.

But I'm at peace with the iron landscape too,
Hard because buildings must be hard to last
— Block, cylinder, cube, built with their angles true,
A dream of righteous permanence, from the past.

In Nixon's era, decades after the ferry,
The copper embodiment of the pieties
Seems hard, but hard like a revolutionary
With indignation, constant as she is.

From here you can glimpse her downstream, her far charm,
Liberty, tiny woman in the mist
— You cannot see the torch — raising her arm
Lorn, bold, as if saluting with her fist.

like a revolutionary. In this description she loses some of her elegance.

Barrow Street Pier, New York
May 1973

He portrays her as she is — a protruding force.

Thomas Bewick

I think of a man on foot
going through thick woods,
a buckle on his brimmed hat,
a stick in his hand.

He comes on from the deep
shadow now to the gladed parts
where light speckles the ground
like scoops out of darkness.

Gnarled branches reaching down
their green gifts; weed reaching up
milky flower and damp leaf.

I think of a man fording
a pebbly stream. A rock
is covered in places with
minute crops of moss
— frail stalks of yellow rising
from the green, each
bloom of it distinct, as
he notices. He notices

the bee's many-jointed legs and its
papery wings veined like leaf,
or the rise of a frog's back
into double peaks, and this morning
by a stile he noticed ferns
afloat on air.

          Drinking from
clear stream and resting
on the rock he loses himself
in detail,
        he reverts
to an earlier self, not yet
separate from what it sees,

a selfless self as difficult
to recover and hold as to
capture the exact way
a burly bluetit grips
its branch (leaning forward)
over this rock
         and in
The History of British Birds.

Autobiography

The sniff of the real, that's
what I'd want to get
     how it felt
to sit on Parliament
Hill on a May evening
studying for exams   skinny
seventeen   dissatisfied
     yet sniffing such
a potent air, smell of
grass in heat from
the day's sun

I'd been walking through the damp
rich ways by the ponds
and now lay on the upper
grass with Lamartine's poems

160

life seemed all
loss, and what was more
I'd lost whatever it was
before I'd even had it

a green dry prospect
distant babble of children
and beyond, distinct at
the end of the glow
St Paul's like a stone thimble

longing so hard to make
inclusions that the longing
has become   in memory
an inclusion *ie normal- this longing is him, part of him.*

NOTES

A MIRROR FOR POETS

The title recalls the book *A Mirror for Magistrates*, conceived in the reign of Henry VIII and reprinted and expanded throughout Elizabeth's reign, the period to which the poem refers. In the original *Mirror* various characters from English history recount in verse their downfalls. The reference to the organization of spies in the first stanza may be to Christopher Marlowe, whom Shakespeare evokes elegiacally in *As You Like It* (III, v, ll. 82–3) and who was a spy.

the Fleet was the common prison while *the Tower* (of London) was reserved for state prisoners.

Ben Jonson (1572–1637), poet and dramatist, killed a fellow actor in a duel in 1598 and escaped death by benefit of clergy, being branded on the thumb instead.

The Earl of Southampton was for a time Elizabeth's powerful favourite.

Arcadia was originally the title of a prose romance (with appended verses) by Sir Philip Sidney; it became the common term for an idealized pastoral world, essentially neo-Platonic in character. This ideal world of *the Forms* contrasts sharply with the reality the poem evokes, and makes reflection on that reality more clear and pointed.

the Paphlagonian King may be Basilius, king of Arcadia in Sidney's book, who falls in love with Pyrocles, a young man who is in turn in love with Basilius's daughter and is disguised as a girl at Basilius's court. Basilius's queen sees through Pyrocles's disguise and falls in love with him as well. Pyrocles gives the king and queen an assignation in a cave on the same night. Basilius is called 'Paphlagonian' to associate him with Paphos (on Cyprus), Aphrodite's home. After many complications, Basilius issues a general pardon ('his huge magnanimity').

pia mater: a delicate inner membrane enveloping brain and spinal cord.

TO YVOR WINTERS, 1955

Yvor Winters (1900–68), the American poet and critic, was Professor of English at Stanford University, California, when Gunn went to study there. This poem records a debt to Winters, evoking the man, his themes, his development and character as they impinge on Gunn himself. The poem recalls in form (though not in tone or in prosodic tact) Winters's own 'Time and the Garden' with its sixteenth- and seventeenth-century models. Winters calls up the toughness of

> Gascoigne, Ben Jonson, Greville, Raleigh, Donne,
> Poets who wrote great poems, one by one,
> And spaced by many years, each line an act
> Through which few labor, which no men retract.

IN SANTA MARIA DEL POPOLO

The church of Santa Maria del Popolo is in the Piazza del Popolo, Rome. The poem supplies such details of the life of Caravaggio, the painter, as are needed, though Gunn follows the legend rather than the facts (Caravaggio was not murdered, though his death was certainly dramatic). Caravaggio is best-known for his brilliant portrayal of sybaritic scenes and his heightened treatment of young flesh. The painting Gunn refers to, 'The Conversion of St Paul', is a masterpiece but not a typical work. Saul was a persecutor of Christians. On the road to Damascus he experienced a miraculous conversion (Acts 9): 'And as he journeyed, he came near Damascus: and suddenly there shined round about him a light from heaven: And he fell to the earth, and heard a voice saying unto him, *Saul, Saul, why persecutest thou me?*' Saul became Paul. His vision left him temporarily blind, but Ananias cured him. Gunn is concerned with the moment of blinding vision, not with its aftermath.

CONSIDERING THE SNAIL

An example of Gunn's syllabic verse, with slant and masculine-feminine rhymes throughout.

THOM GUNN

MY SAD CAPTAINS

Gunn returns to the Shakespearian age for his title and his bearings. The title is from *Antony and Cleopatra* (III, xiii, ll. 181–4). Antony, aware of his impending defeat, speaks:

> Come.
> Let's have one other gaudy night: call to me
> All my sad captains, fill our bowls once more;
> Let's mock the midnight bell.

EPITAPH FOR ANTON SCHMIDT

This poem is part XI of the sequence *Misanthropos*.
  Feldwebel: sergeant.

DIAGRAMS

mesa: a geological formation, a flat-topped outcrop from level land ('mesa' is 'table' in Spanish).

IRON LANDSCAPES (AND THE STATUE OF LIBERTY)

Lackawanna: an American Indian tribe, also the name of an American railway company.

THOMAS BEWICK

This wood engraver (1753–1828), illustrated a number of books but is best remembered for bird and animal engravings, notably *The History of British Birds* (1797, 1804).

AUTOBIOGRAPHY

Parliament Hill Fields, a park in North London, commands a view of the city.
  Alphonse de Lamartine (1790–1859), the French romantic poet and man of affairs, is best remembered for his *Méditations* (1820), which are largely about ephemerality and the loss of love. The poems retain a strong, dubious appeal.

Ted Hughes

Ted Hughes was born in Mytholmroyd, Yorkshire, in 1930. Many of his poems assume the Yorkshire landscape as a backdrop and some – especially the more recent – refer to specific scenes there. When he was seven his family moved to Mexborough and he attended the grammar school. His elder brother became a gamekeeper and his father was a veteran of the First World War. Charles Tomlinson has described the determinants of Hughes's range of poetic reference as 'the mythos of World War I', the European dislocations – cultural, political and psychological – it brought about; and 'an awareness of nature', a fascination with the animal world. In Hughes's mature work these themes have been fused into what must seem a kind of anthropological allegory of ambitious dimensions.

Before going up to Cambridge, Hughes did two years' National Service. During that time he read Shakespeare closely, and his linguistic tap-roots are deep in the Shakespearian age from which he learned certain rhetorical techniques and acquired some of his rare energy. At Cambridge, he began studying English but changed to a course in Archaeology and Anthropology. While at University he met Sylvia Plath whom he married in 1956. He lived for a time in the United States but returned to England in 1959.

Though certain themes dominate Hughes's work, his range of formal experiment is wide. He began by publishing collections of poems, but this format came to seem too narrow: he mingled poetic and prose texts, he prepared libretti, wrote books for children, and in his most recent work has attempted to produce integrated books of verse (in which all the poems relate to an unstated plot) or books with a dark narrative line.

His principal collections are *The Hawk in the Rain* (1957), *Lupercal*

(1960), *Wodwo* (1967), *Crow* (1970), *Season Songs* (1976), *Gaudete* (1977), *Cave Birds* (1978) and *Moortown* (1979). *Selected Poems 1957–1967* and *Selected Poems by Thom Gunn and Ted Hughes* have also been published. In 1971 his selection of Shakespeare, with a particularly illuminating introduction, was published. His works of critical advocacy have included notable introductions to the poetry of Keith Douglas, Emily Dickinson, Vasko Popa, and others. He is a poet remarkably open to forces from the past and from abroad: he has a hungry intelligence and an imagination capable of appropriating what it needs from work it finds congenial.

Hughes reacted against the imaginative narrowness of The Movement, but his own work, for all its energy and inventiveness, suffers from thematic narrowness and from a sameness of tone. Throughout his interesting evolution of forms and styles the unifying factor is a tone and an accent of place which persist even when the poet's scene is not Yorkshire but Devon, or an apocalyptic plain. His development has been an intensification rather than a forward movement. The moral weight of Hughes's work is great: his concern with violence, power and survival has a relevance with which few critics have come to terms – except the terms of ideological dismissal. Hughes is not the simple and elemental poet he is so frequently presented as being. His creaturely world is personalized; and yet his very personal nightmare world is generalized. Aggression and survival in the natural world and in the historical, social world have many aspects, and Hughes's poetry illuminates a range of them while, at the same time, witnessing to the rich particularity of the given world.

The Thought-Fox

I imagine this midnight moment's forest:
Something else is alive
Beside the clock's loneliness
And this blank page where my fingers move.

Through the window I see no star:
Something more near
Though deeper within darkness
Is entering the loneliness:

Cold, delicately as the dark snow
A fox's nose touches twig, leaf;
Two eyes serve a movement, that now
And again now, and now, and now

Sets neat prints into the snow *daunty words match image*
Between trees, and warily a lame
Shadow lags by stump and in hollow
Of a body that is bold to come

Across clearings, an eye,
A widening deepening greenness,
Brilliantly, concentratedly,
Coming about its own business

effect of this line. Till, with a sudden sharp hot stink of fox
It enters the dark hole of the head.
The window is starless still; the clock ticks,
The page is printed.

The Jaguar

The apes yawn and adore their fleas in the sun.
The parrots shriek as if they were on fire, or strut
Like cheap tarts to attract the stroller with the nut.
Fatigued with indolence, tiger and lion

doesn't move — Lie still as the sun. The boa-constrictor's coil
Is a fossil. Cage after cage seems empty, or
Stinks of sleepers from the breathing straw.
It might be painted on a nursery wall.

But who runs like the rest past these arrives
At a cage where the crowd stands, stares, mesmerized,
As a child at a dream, at a jaguar hurrying enraged
Through prison darkness after the drills of his eyes

On a short fierce fuse. Not in boredom –
The eye satisfied to be blind in fire,
By the bang of blood in the brain deaf the ear –
He spins from the bars, but there's no cage to him

More than to the visionary his cell:
His stride is wildernesses of freedom:
The world rolls under the long thrust of his heel.
Over the cage floor the horizons come.

[handwritten: Power of its movement over the poet.]

[handwritten: the movement of The Jaguar gives this impress-ion. admiration / fascination.]

The Horses

I climbed through woods in the hour-before-dawn dark.
Evil air, a frost-making stillness,

[handwritten: elemental]

Not a leaf, not a bird, –
A world cast in frost. I came out above the wood

[handwritten: G. M. Hopkins much influenced by]

Where my breath left tortuous statues in the iron light.
But the valleys were draining the darkness

Till the moorline – blackening dregs of the brightening grey –
Halved the sky ahead. And I saw the horses:

Huge in the dense grey – ten together –
Megalith-still. They breathed, making no move,

With draped manes and tilted hind-hooves,
Making no sound.

I passed: not one snorted or jerked its head.
Grey silent fragments

[handwritten: Solitude - self ?]

Of a grey silent world.

I listened in emptiness on the moor-ridge.
The curlew's tear turned its edge on the silence.

Slowly detail leafed from the darkness. Then the sun
Orange, red, red erupted

Silently, and splitting to its core tore and flung cloud,
Shook the gulf open, showed blue,

[handwritten: good way of describing such massive power, yet silence.]

And the big planets hanging –.
I turned

[handwritten top margin: what he is most aware of in this poem is sound - or lack of it. The only sound is the curlew. That he 'hears' the horizon when there is nothing to hear suggests that here, for him there is something beyond senses]

Stumbling in the fever of a dream, down towards
The dark woods, from the kindling tops,

[handwritten: 'endure' a heavy word. Sense of reluctance.]
[handwritten: burning]

And came to the horses.

                        There, still they stood,
But now steaming and glistening under the flow of light, *[handwritten: detail can be seen]*

Their draped stone manes, their tilted hind-hooves
Stirring under a thaw while all around them

[handwritten: Sun makes it sparkle]

The frost showed its fires. But still they made no sound.
Not one snorted or stamped,

[handwritten: Vivid image - all is alive + burning yet they aren't, a scene which touched the poet.]

Their hung heads patient as the horizons,
High over valleys, in the red levelling rays –

In din of the crowded streets, going among the years, the faces,
May I still meet my memory in so lonely a place

[handwritten left margin: Here in the solitude he met himself]

Between the streams and the red clouds, hearing curlews,
Hearing the horizons endure. *[handwritten: — timelessness]*

[handwritten: and the things which make up himself ie the things which are special to him, have power.]

Wind

This house has been far out at sea all night,
The woods crashing through darkness, the booming hills,
Winds stampeding the fields under the window
Floundering black astride and blinding wet

Till day rose; then under an orange sky
The hills had new places, and wind wielded *[handwritten: Good description of atmosphere of windy day]*
Blade-light, luminous black and emerald,
Flexing like the lens of a mad eye.

At noon I scaled along the house-side as far as
The coal-house door. Once I looked up –
Through the brunt wind that dented the balls of my eyes *[handwritten: Violence]*
The tent of the hills drummed and strained its guyrope,

168

The fields quivering, the skyline a grimace,
At any second to bang and vanish with a flap:
The wind flung a magpie away and a black-
Back gull bent like an iron bar slowly. The house

Rang like some fine green goblet in the note
That any second would shatter it. Now deep
In chairs, in front of the great fire, we grip
Our hearts and cannot entertain book, thought,

Or each other. We watch the fire blazing,
And feel the roots of the house move, but sit on,
Seeing the window tremble to come in,
Hearing the stones cry out under the horizons.

[handwritten annotations: why are they like this? / they fear something — they feel frail, vulnerable, when the wind is this strong? When nature intervenes + makes its presence felt? something they can't control? / warm sense]

October Dawn

October is marigold, and yet
A glass half full of wine left out

To the dark heaven all night, by dawn
Has dreamed a premonition

Of ice across its eye as if
The ice-age had begun its heave.

The lawn overtrodden and strewn
From the night before, and the whistling green

Shrubbery are doomed. Ice
Has got its spearhead into place.

[handwritten annotation: Mortality lack of control]

First a skin, delicately here
Restraining a ripple from the air;

Soon plate and rivet on pond and brook;
Then tons of chain and massive lock

To hold rivers. Then, sound by sight
Will Mammoth and Sabre-tooth celebrate

Reunion while a fist of cold
Squeezes the fire at the core of the world,

Squeezes the fire at the core of the heart,
And now it is about to start.

dread of the cold

Six Young Men

The celluloid of a photograph holds them well, –
Six young men, familiar to their friends.
Four decades that have faded and ochre-tinged
This photograph have not wrinkled the faces or the hands.
Though their cocked hats are not now fashionable,
Their shoes shine. One imparts an intimate smile,
One chews a grass, one lowers his eyes, bashful,
One is ridiculous with cocky pride –
Six months after this picture they were all dead.

Life goes on

All are trimmed for a Sunday jaunt. I know
That bilberried bank, that thick tree, that black wall,
Which are there yet and not changed. From where these sit
You hear the water of seven streams fall
To the roarer in the bottom, and through all
The leafy valley a rumouring of air go.
Pictured here, their expressions listen yet,
And still that valley has not changed its sound
Though their faces are four decades under the ground.

This one was shot in an attack and lay
Calling in the wire, then this one, his best friend,
Went out to bring him in and was shot too;
And this one, the very moment he was warned
From potting at tin-cans in no-man's land,
Fell back dead with his rifle-sights shot away.
The rest, nobody knows what they came to,
But come to the worst they must have done, and held it
Closer than their hope; all were killed.

Here see a man's photograph,
The locket of a smile, turned overnight
Into the hospital of his mangled last
Agony and hours; see bundled in it

His mightier-than-a-man dead bulk and weight:
And on this one place which keeps him alive
(In his Sunday best) see fall war's worst
Thinkable flash and rending, onto his smile
Forty years rotting into soil.

That man's not more alive whom you confront
And shake by the hand, see hale, hear speak loud,
Than any of these six celluloid smiles are,
Nor prehistoric or fabulous beast more dead;
No thought so vivid as their smoking blood:
To regard this photograph might well dement,
Such contradictory permanent horrors here
Smile from the single exposure and shoulder out
One's own body from its instant and heat.

[handwritten: In the photograph, where they are seen alive and smiling from deaths and meaning of death are really brought home. Here they are alive, you can't imagine them dead.]

[handwritten: makes him cold]

Hawk Roosting

I sit in the top of the wood, my eyes closed.
Inaction, no falsifying dream
Between my hooked head and hooked feet:
Or in sleep rehearse perfect kills and eat.

The convenience of the high trees!
The air's buoyancy and the sun's ray
Are of advantage to me;
And the earth's face upward for my inspection.

[handwritten: in control acts as if he commands nature]

My feet are locked upon the rough bark.
It took the whole of Creation
To produce my foot, my each feather:
Now I hold Creation in my foot

Or fly up, and revolve it all slowly –
I kill where I please because it is all mine.
There is no sophistry in my body:
My manners are tearing off heads –

The allotment of death.
For the one path of my flight is direct
Through the bones of the living.
No arguments assert my right:

[handwritten: Conveys character of hawk.]

The sun is behind me.
Nothing has changed since I began.
My eye has permitted no change.
I am going to keep things like this.

[handwritten: conveys idea of control - destroys view of carnivores as acting purely on instinct.]

View Of A Pig

The pig lay on a barrow dead.
It weighed, they said, as much as three men.
Its eyes closed, pink white eyelashes.
Its trotters stuck straight out.

Such weight and thick pink bulk
Set in death seemed not just dead.
It was less than lifeless, further off.
It was like a sack of wheat.

I thumped it without feeling remorse.
One feels guilty insulting the dead,
Walking on graves. But this pig
Did not seem able to accuse.

It was too dead. Just so much
A poundage of lard and pork.
Its last dignity had entirely gone.
It was not a figure of fun.

Too dead now to pity.
To remember its life, din, stronghold
Of earthly pleasure as it had been,
Seemed a false effort, and off the point.

Too deadly factual. Its weight
Oppressed me – how could it be moved?
And the trouble of cutting it up!
The gash in its throat was shocking, but not pathetic.

Once I ran at a fair in the noise
To catch a greased piglet
That was faster and nimbler than a cat,
Its squeal was the rending of metal.

TED HUGHES

Pigs must have hot blood, they feel like ovens.
Their bite is worse than a horse's –
They chop a half-moon clean out.
They eat cinders, dead cats.

Distinctions and admirations such
As this one was long finished with.
I stared at it a long time. They were going to scald it,
Scald it and scour it like a doorstep.

[handwritten top margin: Thrushes- art must be so swift a reflex of personality that it strikes unerringly for the mark as if purely instinctual]

[handwritten: Contrast between the pig alive and the pig dead. But he doesn't use the same pig for as he says, the first one never seemed to be alive.]

Thrushes

[handwritten: ie attentive]

Terrifying are the attent sleek thrushes on the lawn,
More coiled steel than living – a poised
Dark deadly eye, those delicate legs
Triggered to stirrings beyond sense – with a start, a bounce, a stab
Overtake the instant and drag out some writhing thing.
No indolent procrastinations and no yawning stares.
No sighs or head-scratchings. Nothing but bounce and stab
And a ravening second.

[handwritten right: religion incapacitates man. It 'distracts' him.]

[handwritten: anti poetic thrush]

Is it their single-mind-sized skulls, or a trained
Body, or a genius, or a nestful of brats
Gives their days this bullet and automatic
Purpose? Mozart's brain had it, and the shark's mouth
That hungers down the blood-smell even to a leak of its own
Side and devouring of itself: efficiency which
Strikes too streamlined for any doubt to pluck at it
Or obstruction deflect.

[handwritten: no gap between thought + action, there acts don't worship themselves.]

[handwritten: art through moral 'myths'- Praises vital energy / mad. images of good + bad ie. it is irrelevant to the importance of life itself, it is up a pointless act]

With a man it is otherwise. Heroisms on horseback,
Outstripping his desk-diary at a broad desk,
Carving at a tiny ivory ornament
For years: his act worships itself – while for him,
Though he bends to be blent in prayer, how loud and above what
Furious spaces of fire do the distracting devils
Orgy and hosannah, under what wilderness
Of black silent waters weep.

[handwritten: mocking man.]

[handwritten: blended]

[handwritten: how far away from him they are.]

[handwritten bottom: who know why they are here - instinct survival]

[handwritten: man's ordinary life has little meaning/purpose as opposed to animals]

[handwritten: As animals go about their lives they are aware of them, ie mortality, they live properly. We do not.]

173

Her Husband

Comes home dull with coal-dust deliberately
To grime the sink and foul towels and let her
Learn with scrubbing brush and scrubbing board
The stubborn character of money.

And let her learn through what kind of dust
He has earned his thirst and the right to quench it
And what sweat he has exchanged for his money
And the blood-weight of money. He'll humble her

With new light on her obligations.
The fried, woody chips, kept warm two hours in the oven,
Are only part of her answer.
Hearing the rest, he slams them to the fire back

And is away round the house-end singing
'Come back to Sorrento' in a voice
Of resounding corrugated iron.
Her back has bunched into a hump as an insult.

God/fate etc doesn't want to know. There is no answer. This is just the way things are.

For they will have their rights.
Their jurors are to be assembled *he from the coal he digs.*
From the little crumbs of soot. Their brief
Goes straight up to heaven and nothing more is heard of it.

Totally private

Prowler / predator

The Green Wolf *Death?*

Your neighbour moves less and less, attempts less.
If his right hand still moves, it is a farewell
Already days posthumous.

But the left hand seems to freeze,
And the left leg with its crude plumbing,
And the left half jaw and the left eyelid and the words all
the huge cries

174

Frozen in his brain his tongue cannot unfreeze –
While somewhere through a dark heaven
The dark bloodclot moves in.

You watch it approaching but you cannot fear it.
The punctual evening star, *Death.*
Worse, the warm hawthorn blossoms, their foam,

Their palls of deathly perfume, *hawthorn is bad luck, also sickly perfume.*
Worst of all the beanflower
Badged with jet like the ear of the tiger *seasons- always coming round again. Not so for humanity*

Unmake and remake you. That star
And that flower and that flower
And living mouth and living mouth all *Life in a sense kills death*

One smouldering annihilation
Of old brains, old bowels, old bodies
In the scarves of dew, the wet hair of nightfall. *heaviness, suffocating sense* *wet hair has odour, as does nightfall.*

Out

I
The Dream Time

My father sat in his chair recovering
From the four-year mastication by gunfire and mud,
Body buffeted wordless, estranged by long soaking
In the colours of mutilation.
                              His outer perforations
Were valiantly healed, but he and the hearth-fire, its blood-flicker
On biscuit-bowl and piano and table leg,
Moved into strong and stronger possession *domestication contrast with war images.*
Of minute after minute, as the clock's tiny cog
Laboured and on the thread of his listening
Dragged him bodily from under
The mortised four-year strata of dead Englishmen
He belonged with. He felt his limbs clearing *It is dragging him back but he belongs there - guilt*
With every slight, gingerish movement. While I, small and four, *at being alive.*
Lay on the carpet as his luckless double, *both growing up in different ways*
His memory's buried, immovable anchor,
Among jawbones and blown-off boots, tree-stumps, shellcases
                              and craters,

Under rain that goes on drumming its rods and thickening
Its kingdom, which the sun has abandoned, and where nobody
Can ever again move from shelter.

ie none of them can get out, survivors or not.

II

The dead man in his cave beginning to sweat;
The melting bronze visor of flesh
Of the mother in the baby-furnace –
Nobody believes, it
Could be nothing, all
Undergo smiling at
The lulling of blood in
Their ears, their ears, their ears, their eyes
Are only drops of water and even the dead man suddenly
Sits up and sneezes – Atishoo!
Then the nurse wraps him up, smiling,
And, though faintly, the mother is smiling,
And it's just another baby. *It's never just another baby, it's somebody's child.*

death and birth and re-birth [His father]

As after being blasted to bits
The reassembled infantryman
Tentatively totters out, gazing around with the eyes
Of an exhausted clerk. *Implies innocence, youth.*

III

Remembrance Day *Puts a different light on things*

The poppy is a wound, the poppy is the mouth
Of the grave, maybe of the womb searching –

A canvas-beauty puppet on a wire
Today whoring everywhere. It is years since I wore one.

It is more years
The shrapnel that shattered my father's paybook

Gripped me, and all his dead
Gripped him to a time

He no more than they could outgrow, but, cast into one, like iron,
Hung deeper than refreshing of ploughs

In the woe-dark under my mother's eye –
One anchor

Holding my juvenile neck bowed to the dunkings of the Atlantic.
So goodbye to that bloody-minded flower.

He is tied to it by his father's + mother's suffering

You dead bury your dead.
Goodbye to the cenotaphs on my mother's breasts.

Goodbye to all the remaindered charms of my father's survival.
Let England close. Let the green sea-anemone close.

England put his father here, 'ate' all those who died. Poppies etc. are a way of assauging guilt.

an open sea anemone eats things up.

Kafka

> And he is an owl
> He is an owl, 'Man' tattooed in his armpit
> Under the broken wing
> (Stunned by the wall of glare, he fell here)
> Under the broken wing of huge shadow that twitches
> across the floor.

> He is a man in hopeless feathers.

Full Moon and Little Frieda

A cool small evening shrunk to a dog bark and the clank of a
bucket –

And you listening.
A spider's web, tense for the dew's touch.
A pail lifted, still and brimming – mirror
To tempt a first star to a tremor.

tension. sense of an instant held in time.

Cows are going home in the lane there, looping the
hedges with their warm wreaths of breath –
A dark river of blood, many boulders,
Balancing unspilled milk.

potential hazards

'Moon!' you cry suddenly, 'Moon! Moon!'

The moon has stepped back like an artist gazing amazed at a work
That points at him amazed. *attempting to communicate the strangeness of the world. What we don't know about it.*

amazed at her le the creation, his daughter.

Wodwo
wood dweller or wood demon,

What am I? Nosing here, turning leaves over *no one is sure*
Following a faint stain on the air to the river's edge *which*
I enter water. What am I to split
The glassy grain of water looking upward I see the bed
Of the river above me upside down very clear
What am I doing here in mid-air? Why do I find
this frog so interesting as I inspect its most secret
interior and make it my own? Do these weeds
know me and name me to each other have they
seen me before, do I fit in their world? I seem
separate from the ground and not rooted but dropped
out of nothing casually I've no threads
fastening me to anything I can go anywhere
I seem to have been given the freedom
of this place what am I then? And picking
bits of bark off this rotten stump gives me
no pleasure and it's no use so why do I do it
me and doing that have coincided very queerly
But what shall I be called am I the first
have I an owner what shape am I what
shape am I am I huge if I go
to the end on this way past these trees and past these trees
till I get tired that's touching one wall of me
for the moment if I sit still how everything
stops to watch me I suppose I am the exact centre
but there's all this what is it roots
roots roots roots and here's the water
again very queer but I'll go on looking

comic comment on the hawklike mentality, deflating earlier poetic endeavours.

height of self awareness and awareness of surroundings, and relation of oneself with them

prelude to Crow poems - the humour especially

Examination at the Womb-door

Who owns these scrawny little feet? *Death.*
Who owns this bristly scorched-looking face? *Death.*
Who owns these still-working lungs? *Death.*
Who owns this utility coat of muscles? *Death.*
Who owns these unspeakable guts? *Death.*
Who owns these questionable brains? *Death.*
All this messy blood? *Death.*
These minimum-efficiency eyes? *Death.*
This wicked little tongue? *Death.*
This occasional wakefulness? *Death.*

Given, stolen, or held pending trial?
Held.

Who owns the whole rainy, stony earth? *Death.*
Who owns all of space? *Death.*

Who is stronger than hope? *Death.*
Who is stronger than the will? *Death.*
Stronger than love? *Death.*
Stronger than life? *Death.*

But who is stronger than death?
Me, evidently.

Pass, Crow.

[handwritten annotations: "description of a foetus"; "+ Understands the consequences of death being supreme"; "Because he recognises death being supreme"; "Crow is the arch-survivor."]

Crow Alights

Crow saw the herded mountains, steaming in the morning.
And he saw the sea
Dark-spined, with the whole earth in its coils.
He saw the stars, fuming away into the black, mushrooms of the
        nothing forest, clouding their spores, the virus of God.

And he shivered with the horror of Creation.

179

In the hallucination of the horror
He saw this shoe, with no sole, rain-sodden,
Lying on a moor. *'street wise.'*
And there was this garbage can, bottom rusted away,
A playing place for the wind, in a waste of puddles.

There was this coat, in the dark cupboard, in the silent room, in
                                   the silent house.
There was this face, smoking its cigarette between the dusk
                            window and the fire's embers.

Near the face, this hand, motionless.

Near the hand, this cup.

Crow blinked.   He blinked.   Nothing faded.

He stared at the evidence.

Nothing escaped him. (Nothing could escape.)

*if Crow understands
all about death
he vouches all that
he sees with
mortality*

Crow and the Birds

*they all
avoid
humanity.*

When the eagle soared clear through a dawn distilling of emerald
When the curlew trawled in seadusk through a chime of
                              wineglasses
When the swallow swooped through a woman's song in a cavern
And the swift flicked through the breath of a violet

When the owl sailed clear of tomorrow's conscience
And the sparrow preened himself of yesterday's promise
And the heron laboured clear of the Bessemer upglare
And the bluetit zipped clear of lace panties
And the woodpecker drummed clear of the rotovator and the
                              rose-farm
And the peewit tumbled clear of the laundromat

While the bullfinch plumped in the apple bud
And the goldfinch bulbed in the sun
And the wryneck crooked in the moon
And the dipper peered from the dewball

*Crow
exploits it.*

Crow spraddled head-down in the beach-garbage, guzzling a
                              dropped ice-cream.

Crow's Last Stand

Burning
     burning
          burning
                    there was finally something
The sun could not burn, that it had rendered
Everything down to – a final obstacle
Against which it raged and charred

And rages and chars

Limpid among the glaring furnace clinkers
The pulsing blue tongues and the red and the yellow
The green lickings of the conflagration

Limpid and black –

Crow's eye-pupil, in the tower of its scorched fort.

Apple Dumps

After the fiesta, the beauty-contests, the drunken wrestling
Of the blossom
Come some small ugly swellings, the dwarfish truths
Of the prizes.

After blushing and confetti, the breeze-blown bridesmaids, the
                              shadowed snapshots
Of the trees in bloom
Come the gruelling knuckles, and the cracked housemaid's hands,
The workworn morning plainness of apples.

sees the tree through human association/ vision.

Unearthly was the hope, the wet star melting the gland,
Staggering the offer –
But pawky the real returns, not easy to see,
Dull and leaf-green, hidden, still-bitter, and hard.

Hope.

The orchard flared wings, like a new heaven, a dawn-lipped
                                                    apocalypse
Kissing the sleeper –
The apples emerge, in the sun's black shade, among stricken trees,
A straggle of survivors, nearly all ailing.

The River in March

Now the river is rich, but her voice is low.
It is her Mighty Majesty the sea
Travelling among the villages incognito.

Now the river is poor. No song, just a thin mad whisper.
The winter floods have ruined her.
She squats between draggled banks, fingering her rags and
                                                    rubbish.

And now the river is rich. A deep choir.
It is the lofty clouds, that work in heaven,
Going on their holiday to the sea.

The river is poor again. All her bones are showing.
Through a dry wig of bleached flotsam she peers up ashamed
From her slum of sticks.

Now the river is rich, collecting shawls and minerals.
Rain brought fatness, but she takes ninety-nine percent
Leaving the fields just one percent to survive on.

And now she is poor. Now she is East wind sick.
She huddles in holes and corners. The brassy sun gives her a
                                                    headache.
She has lost all her fish. And she shivers.

But now once more she is rich. She is viewing her lands.
A hoard of king-cups spills from her folds, it blazes, it cannot be
                                                    hidden.

A salmon, a sow of solid silver,

Bulges to glimpse it.

a sort of consumation

a confirmation of its riches.

river dominating the land.

NOTES

THE THOUGHT-FOX

There is clearly a debt in the first line to Gerard Manley Hopkins's 'The Windhover' which starts: 'I caught this morning morning's minion, kingdom of daylight's dauphin, . . .'

WIND

Conceptually, this poem may owe something to Louis MacNeice's 'House on a Cliff'.

THRUSHES

The first line recalls to my mind Emily Dickinson's 'Presentiment – is that long Shadow – on the lawn'. Hughes introduced a selection of her poems, and the diction here and elsewhere in the early work has that elaborated quality with which she is associated ('indolent procrastinations', 'ravening second', etc.) though of course Hughes is in pursuit of different prosodic and thematic ends.

OUT

The poet's father saw active service in the First World War.

KAFKA

Originally this poem, called 'Kafka Writes', was part two of the sequence 'Wings' (Sartre and Einstein were subjects of parts one and three respectively). The radically innovative Czech novelist and writer Franz Kafka (1883–1924) is best known for his novels *The Castle* and *The Trial*. ('Kafka', in Czech, means 'crow'.)

FULL MOON AND LITTLE FRIEDA

Frieda: the poet's daughter.

WODWO

In the Middle English poem *Sir Gawayne and the Grene Knight*, 'wodwos' are wood-dwellers or wood-demons of some sort – scholars cannot agree about their nature, and Hughes's wodwo isn't sure either. Sir Gawayne's travails with the wodwos are briefly alluded to in these lines:

Sumwhile with wormes he werres, and with wolves als,
Sumwhile with wodwos, that woned in the knarres.

EXAMINATION AT THE WOMB-DOOR

This and the three poems that follow it are from a sequence of sixty
poems entitled *Crow*. Crow is the arch-survivor.

CROW AND THE BIRDS

Bessemer upglare: the Bessemer process, a way of making steel from
cast iron using a blast furnace and a Bessemer converter.

CROW'S LAST STAND

The opening words recall T. S. Eliot's *The Waste Land* (the closing
passage of 'The Fire Sermon'). Hughes acknowledges a considerable
debt to Eliot. In his mature work it is conceptual rather than
prosodic, and clearly a debt to the poet of *The Waste Land*, the
'Sweeney' poems, and other early work, not to the poet of *Four
Quartets*.

Geoffrey Hill

Geoffrey Hill was born in Bromsgrove, Worcester, in 1932. In 1950 he went to Oxford to read English. He became a lecturer and eventually Professor of English at Leeds University.

In 1952, when he was twenty, The Fantasy Press issued a pamphlet containing five poems, among them was 'Genesis' (p. 186), one of his finest achievements. Originally it bore the dedication 'A Ballad to Christopher Smart'. That first collection recorded debts to other poets: to the Scottish Chaucerians; to Isaac Rosenberg, the outstanding First World War poet; to Blake; to Chaucer. One can also detect debts to Keith Douglas. Hill chose exacting masters. In rejecting The Movement, he turned not to the romantic poets of the 1940s but to the neglected tradition represented by Douglas. In putting down his roots in the past, he found his most congenial soil in the fourteenth and fifteenth centuries and in the late-eighteenth century. Though his later work shows him closely acquainted with the English literature of the sixteenth and seventeenth centuries as well, and with the crucial historical struggles of those times, his imagination has detected a tradition quite distinct from Eliot's or from that prescribed by The Movement poets. When Hill is baroque, as he often is in his mature work, we are not put in mind of Donne but – perhaps – of Dunbar, that dazzling craftsman, or of the baroque poets of Spain. Hill's work has profited from his acquaintance (direct or from translation) with the Spanish tradition from Lope de Vega to Lorca.

Like Hughes, he is concerned with power, but he explores it through history and not through myth. He explores it from the perspective of the powerful – the empowered – and the powerless – the victim. Power need not be only political: there is also the power of love, and the poems in the 'Arrurruz' sequence (p. 194) vividly explore this theme. The elegies to poets and to other victims of war and repression are among Hill's finest achievements. There are, too, the poems in which the poet examines his conscience in times of trouble and repression or in their aftermath. Throughout the poems there is a religious current as well, no less powerful for its ambivalence.

Geoffrey Hill has published four major collections: *For the Unfallen: Poems 1952–1958* (1959), *King Log* (1968), *Mercian Hymns* (1971) and *Tenebrae* (1978). Selection from *Mercian Hymns*, canticles or 'prose poems' which form an inviolable unity, baffled me, and I have included nothing from that book. I was unwilling to do violence to the text. I have, however, included what I take to be a major poem of our time, 'The Pentecost Castle' sequence, in which Hill achieves effects not found elsewhere in English poetry. The spareness and precision of the writing and the fluidity of the syntax recall the finest work of the Spanish 'Golden Age'.

The formal versatility of Hill's work is extraordinary. As in the work of Ted Hughes, one finds that the common element in all the poems is their tone. Hill's jokes are grim. Darkness, blood and death are seldom absent from the work. This insistent, somewhat narrow, current of concern runs deep, however. Some critics complain about the deliberate (some say over-deliberate) nature of the writing, especially in the long-lined poems, the veritable cramming of every rift with ore. They feel the poetry is stifled in a kind of absolute verbal control. Other critics and readers find this verbal control – which at times is capable of amazing lightness as well as of serious deliberation – a rare virtue in modern poetry.

Genesis

I

Against the burly air I strode,
Where the tight ocean heaves its load,
Crying the miracles of God.

And first I brought the sea to bear
Upon the dead weight of the land;
And the waves flourished at my prayer,
The rivers spawned their sand.

And where the streams were salt and full
The tough pig-headed salmon strove,
Curbing the ebb and the tide's pull,
To reach the steady hills above.

II

The second day I stood and saw
The osprey plunge with triggered claw,
Feathering blood along the shore,
To lay the living sinew bare.

And the third day I cried: 'Beware
The soft-voiced owl, the ferret's smile,
The hawk's deliberate stoop in air,
Cold eyes, and bodies hooped in steel,
Forever bent upon the kill.'

III

And I renounced, on the fourth day,
This fierce and unregenerate clay,

Building as a huge myth for man
The watery Leviathan,

And made the glove-winged albatross
Scour the ashes of the sea
Where Capricorn and Zero cross,
A brooding immortality –
Such as the charmed phoenix has
In the unwithering tree.

IV

The phoenix burns as cold as frost;
And, like a legendary ghost,
The phantom-bird goes wild and lost,
Upon a pointless ocean tossed.

So, the fifth day, I turned again
To flesh and blood and the blood's pain.

V

On the sixth day, as I rode
In haste about the works of God,
With spurs I plucked the horse's blood.

By blood we live, the hot, the cold,
To ravage and redeem the world:
There is no bloodless myth will hold.

And by Christ's blood are men made free
Though in close shrouds their bodies lie
Under the rough pelt of the sea;

Though Earth has rolled beneath her weight
The bones that cannot bear the light.

1952

Merlin

I will consider the outnumbering dead:
For they are the husks of what was rich seed.
Now, should they come together to be fed,
They would outstrip the locusts' covering tide.

Arthur, Elaine, Mordred; they are all gone
Among the raftered galleries of bone.
By the long barrows of Logres they are made one,
And over their city stands the pinnacled corn.

1953

The White Ship

Where the living with effort go,
Or with expense, the drowned wander
Easily: seaman
And king's son also

Who, by gross error lost,
Drift, now, in salt crushed
Polyp- and mackerel-fleshed
Tides between coast and coast,

Submerge or half-appear.
This does not much matter.
They are put down as dead. Water
Silences all who would interfere;

Retains, still, what it might give
As casually as it took away:
Creatures passed through the wet sieve
Without enrichment or decay.

1956

Doctor Faustus

> For it must needs be that
> offences come; but woe to
> that man by whom the
> offence cometh.

I *The Emperor's Clothes*

A way of many ways: a god
Spirals in the pure steam of blood.
And gods – as men – rise from shut tombs
To a disturbance of small drums;

Immaculate plumage of the swan
The common wear. There is no-one
Afraid or overheard, no loud
Voice (though innocently loud).

II *The Harpies*

Having stood hungrily apart
From the gods' politic banquet,
Of all possible false gods
I fall to these gristled shades

That show everything, without lust;
And stumble upon their dead feast
By the torn *Warning To Bathers*
By the torn waters.

    III *Another Part of the Fable*

The Innocents have not flown;
Too legendary, they laugh;
The lewd uproarious wolf
Brings their house down.

A beast is slain, a beast thrives.
Fat blood squeaks on the sand.
A blinded god believes
That he is not blind.

1958

To the (Supposed) Patron

Prodigal of loves and barbecues,
Expert in the strangest faunas, at home
He considers the lilies, the rewards.
There is no substitute for a rich man.
At his first entering a new province
With new coin, music, the barest glancing
Of steel or gold suffices. There are many
Tremulous dreams secured under that head.
For his delight and his capacity
To absorb, freshly, the inside-succulence
Of untoughened sacrifice, his bronze agents
Speculate among convertible stones
And drink desert sand. That no mirage
Irritate his mild gaze, the lewd noonday
Is housed in cool places, and fountains
Salt the sparse haze. His flesh is made clean.
For the unfallen – the firstborn, or wise
Councillor – prepared vistas extend
As far as harvest; and idyllic death
Where fish at dawn ignite the powdery lake.

1958

Ovid in the Third Reich

non peccat, quaecumque potest peccasse negare,
solaque famosam culpa professa facit.
(AMORES, III, xiv)

I love my work and my children. God
Is distant, difficult. Things happen.
Too near the ancient troughs of blood
Innocence is no earthly weapon.

I have learned one thing: not to look down
So much upon the damned. They, in their sphere,
Harmonize strangely with the divine
Love. I, in mine, celebrate the love-choir.

September Song

born 19.6.32 – deported 24.9.42

Undesirable you may have been, untouchable
you were not. Not forgotten
or passed over at the proper time.

As estimated, you died. Things marched,
sufficient, to that end.
Just so much Zyklon and leather, patented
terror, so many routine cries.

(I have made
an elegy for myself it
is true)

September fattens on vines. Roses
flake from the wall. The smoke
of harmless fires drifts to my eyes.

This is plenty. This is more than enough.

Four Poems Regarding the Endurance of Poets

MEN ARE A MOCKERY OF ANGELS
i.m. Tommaso Campanella, priest and poet

Some days a shadow through
The high window shares my
Prison. I watch a slug
Scale the glinting pit-side
Of its own slime. The cries
As they come are mine; then
God's: my justice, wounds, love,
Derisive light, bread, filth.

To lie here in my strange
Flesh while glutted Torment
Sleeps, stained with its prompt food,
Is a joy past all care
Of the world, for a time.
But we are commanded
To rise, when, in silence,
I would compose my voice.

A PRAYER TO THE SUN
i.m. Miguel Hernandez

i
Darkness
above all things
the Sun
makes
rise   ii
Vultures
salute their meat
at noon
(Hell is
silent)   iii
Blind Sun
our ravager
bless us
so that
we sleep.

'DOMAINE PUBLIC'
i.m. Robert Desnos, died Terezin Camp, 1945

For reading I can recommend
   the Fathers. How they
cultivate the corrupting flesh:

toothsome contemplation: cleanly
   maggots churning spleen
to milk. For exercise, prolonged

suppression of much improper
   speech from proper tombs.
If the ground opens, should men's mouths

open also? 'I am nothing
   if not saved now!' or
'Christ, what a pantomime!' The days

of the week are seven pits. Look,
   Seigneur, again we
resurrect and the judges come.

TRISTIA: 1891–1938
A Valediction to Osip Mandelshtam

Difficult friend, I would have preferred
You to them. The dead keep their sealed lives
And again I am too late. Too late
The salutes, dust-clouds and brazen cries.

Images rear from desolation
Look . . . ruins upon a plain . . .
A few men glare at their hands; others
Grovel for food in the roadside field.

Tragedy has all under regard.
It will not touch us but it is there –
Flawless, insatiate – hard summer sky
Feasting on this, reaching its own end.

from *The Songbook of Sebastian Arrurruz*

I

Ten years without you. For so it happens.
Days make their steady progress, a routine
That is merciful and attracts nobody.

Already, like a disciplined scholar,
I piece fragments together, past conjecture
Establishing true sequences of pain;

For so it is proper to find value
In a bleak skill, as in the thing restored:
The long-lost words of choice and valediction.

COPLAS

i

'One cannot lose what one has not possessed'.
So much for that abrasive gem.
I can lose what I want. I want you.

ii

Oh my dear one, I shall grieve for you
For the rest of my life with slightly
Varying cadence, oh my dear one.

iii

Half-mocking the half-truth, I note
'The wild brevity of sensual love'.
I am shaken, even by that.

iv

It is to him I write, it is to her
I speak in contained silence. Will they be touched
By the unfamiliar passion between them?

3

What other men do with other women
Is for me neither orgy nor sacrament
Nor a language of foreign candour

But is mere occasion or chance distance
Out of which you might move and speak my name
As I speak yours, bargaining with sleep's

Miscellaneous gods for as much
As I can have: an alien landscape,
The dream where you are always to be found.

4

A workable fancy. Old petulant
Sorrow comes back to us, metamorphosed
And semi-precious. Fortuitous amber.
As though this recompensed our deprivation.
See how each fragment kindles as we turn it,
At the end, into the light of appraisal.

5

Love, oh my love, it will come
Sure enough! A storm
Broods over the dry earth all day.
At night the shutters throb in its downpour.

The metaphor holds; is a snug house.
You are outside, lost somewhere. I find myself
Devouring verses of stranger passion
And exile. The exact words

Are fed into my blank hunger for you.

Postures

I imagine, as I imagine us
Each time more stylized more lovingly
Detailed, that I am not myself
But someone I might have been: sexless,
Indulgent about art, relishing
Let us say the well-schooled
Postures of *St Anthony* or *St Jerome*,
Those peaceful hermaphrodite dreams
Through which the excess of memory
Pursues its own abstinence.

The Pentecost Castle

It is terrible to desire and not
possess, and terrible to possess
and not desire.
W. B. YEATS

What we love in other human
beings is the hoped-for satisfaction
of our desire. We do not love their
desire. If what we loved in them
was their desire, then we should
love them as ourself.
SIMONE WEIL

I

They slew by night
upon the road
Medina's pride
Olmedo's flower

shadows warned him
not to go
not to go
along that road

weep for your lord
Medina's pride
Olmedo's flower
there in the road

2

Down in the orchard
I met my death
under the briar rose
I lie slain

I was going
to gather flowers
my love waited
among the trees

down in the orchard
I met my death
under the briar rose
I lie slain

3

You watchers on the wall
grown old with care
I too looked from the wall
I shall look no more

tell us what you saw
the lord I sought to serve
caught in the thorn grove
his blood on his brow

you keepers of the wall
what friend or enemy
sets free the cry
of the bell

4

At dawn the Mass
burgeons from stone
a Jesse tree
of resurrection

budding with candle
flames the gold
and the white wafers
of the feast

and ghosts for love
void a few tears
of wax upon
forlorn altars

5

Goldfinch and hawk
and the grey aspen tree
I have run to the river
mother call me home

the leaves glint in the wind
turning their quiet song
the wings flash and are still
I sleep in the shade

when I cried out you
made no reply
tonight I shall pass by
without a sound

6

Slowly my heron flies
pierced by the blade
mounting in slow pain
strikes the air with its cries

goes seeking the high rocks
where no man can climb
where the wild balsam stirs
by the little stream

the rocks the high rocks
are brimming with flowers
there love grows and there love
rests and is saved

7

I went out early
to the far field
ermine and lily
and yet a child

Love stood before me
in that place
prayers could not lure me
to Christ's house

Christ the deceiver
took all I had
his darkness ever
my fair reward

8

And you my spent heart's treasure
my yet unspent desire
measurer past all measure
cold paradox of fire

as seeker so forsaken
consentingly denied
your solitude a token
the sentries at your side

fulfilment to my sorrow
indulgence of your prey
the sparrowhawk the sparrow
the nothing that you say

9

This love will see me dead
he has the place in mind
where I am free to die
be true at last true love

my love meet me half-way
I bear no sword of fear
where you dwell I
dwell also says my lord

dealing his five wounds
so cunning and so true
of love to rouse this death
I die to sleep in love

10

St James and St John
bless the road she has gone
St John and St James
a rosary of names

child-beads of fingered bread
never-depleted heart's food
the nominal the real
subsistence past recall

bread we shall never break
love-runes we cannot speak
scrolled effigy of a cry
our passion its display

11

If the night is dark
and the way short
why do you hold back
dearest heart

though I may never
see you again
touch me I will shiver
at the unseen

the night is so dark
the way so short
why do you not break
o my heart

12

Married and not for love
you of all women
you of all women
my soul's darling my love

faithful to my desire
lost in the dream's grasp where
shall I find you everywhere
unmatched in my desire

each of us dispossessed
so richly in my sleep
I rise out of my sleep
crying like one possessed

13

Splendidly-shining darkness
proud citadel of meekness
likening us our unlikeness
majesty of our distress

emptiness ever thronging
untenable belonging
how long until this longing
end in unending song

and soul for soul discover
no strangeness to dissever
and lover keep with lover
a moment and for ever

14

As he is wounded
I am hurt
he bleeds from pride
I from my heart

as he is dying
I shall live
in grief desiring
still to grieve

as he is living
I shall die
sick of forgiving
such honesty

I shall go down
to the lovers' well
and wash this wound
that will not heal

beloved soul
what shall you see
nothing at all
yet eye to eye

depths of non-being
perhaps too clear
my desire dying
as I desire

Two Chorale-Preludes
on melodies by Paul Celan

I   AVE REGINA COELORUM

Es ist ein Land Verloren . . .

There is a land called Lost
at peace inside our heads.
The moon, full on the frost,
vivifies these stone heads.

Moods of the verb 'to stare',
split selfhoods, conjugate
ice-facets from the air,
the light glazing the light.

Look at us, Queen of Heaven!
Our solitudes drift by
your solitudes, the seven
dead stars in your sky.

GEOFFREY HILL

2   TE LUCIS ANTE TERMINUM

Wir gehen dir, Heimat, ins Garn . . .

Centaury with your staunch bloom
you there alder beech you fern,
midsummer closeness my far home,
fresh traces of lost origin.

Silvery the black cherries hang,
the plum-tree oozes through each cleft
and horse-flies siphon the green dung,
glued to the sweetness of their graft:

immortal transience, a 'kind
of otherness', self-understood,
BE FAITHFUL grows upon the mind
as lichen glimmers on the wood.

NOTES

GENESIS

Originally the poem was sub-titled 'A Ballad to Christopher Smart'.
The five sections follow a seven-day development (the seventh,
Sabbath, remains unstated). It is the 'genesis' of an understanding of
the implicit cruelty of the world, an awareness of the character of
Christian truth (without final commitment to it), developed in terms
parallel to those of the Genesis creation story. The poem traces the
development of an individual consciousness and a particular country's history and culture through its language, by Hill's deft use of
archaic and period syntax and diction. In the third section the speaker
rejects earth ('clay') and builds a myth based on the other three
elements, water, air and fire, represented by imaginary creatures
appropriate to each, and suitably remote from the literal creatures
elsewhere in the poem.
    stoop: the hawk's swooping down on its quarry or lure
(Elizabethan usage).
    Leviathan: huge sea monster; also the title of Thomas Hobbes's
great political treatise, hence – though here distantly – the state.

MERLIN

The soothsayer-wizard and counsellor to King Arthur.

Elaine: the 'fair maid of Astolat' (cf. Malory).
Mordred: Arthur's usurping son.
Logres: Loegria, used by Geoffrey of Monmouth (1100?–1154) to refer to those parts of Britain assigned to King Locrine; by Spenser to refer to England itself.

DOCTOR FAUSTUS

The epigraph is from Matthew 18.7 (Authorised Version). Christ tells his disciples they must become as little children, and that

who so shall offend one of these little ones which believe in me, it were better for him that a millstone were hanged about his neck, and that he were drowned in the depth of the sea. Woe unto the world because of offences! for it must needs be that offences come; but woe to that man by whom the offence cometh! Wherefore if thy hand or thy foot offend thee, cut them off, and cast them from thee: it is better for thee to enter into life halt or maimed, rather than having two hands or two feet to be cast into everlasting fire.

The appositeness of this passage and its sequel to Hill's poem is clear.

OVID IN THE THIRD REICH

The epigraph, in Christopher Marlowe's translation, reads:

She hath not trod awry that doth deny it,
Such as confess have lost their good names by it.

SEPTEMBER SONG

The poet himself was born in 1932.
Zyklon: lethal gas crystals used by the Nazis in the extermination camps.

FOUR POEMS REGARDING THE ENDURANCE OF POETS

Tommaso Campanella (1568–1639), Italian theologian, philosopher and poet, was persecuted for his Telesian views by his own order (the Dominicans) and then by the Inquisition. He was politically active as well.

Miguel Hernandez, the Spanish peasant-poet, a Republican volunteer in the Civil War, was eventually imprisoned in Alicante where he died of tuberculosis.

Robert Desnos (1900–45), the French surrealist poet and novelist, died of starvation and typhus after being imprisoned by the Nazis for Resistance activities. *Domaine Public* was a posthumous representative collection of his poetry (1953).

Osip Mandelshtam (1892?–1938), a leading Russian poet, critic and translator, starved on the way to one of Stalin's death-camps. His poem 'Tristia' (1918) begins: 'I have mastered the science of farewells'.

from THE SONGBOOK OF SEBASTIAN ARRURRUZ

Sebastian Arrurruz ('Sebastian shot through with arrows') was an apocryphal Spanish poet ('1868–1922') whose 'songbook' Hill devises in the 'cancionero' tradition of Spanish poetry.

Coplas: a Spanish poetic form with a long and varied history: Hill's own use resembles that of Antonio Machado (1875–1939), though thematically and tonally the poems are Hill's own.

THE PENTECOST CASTLE

At Pentecost the Holy Spirit visited the Apostles as a tongue of flame and they received the gift of tongues to spread the Word. The poet takes much of his imagery and the short, fluid line from a reading of *El Caballero de Olmedo*, a revenge tragedy by the Spanish Golden Age dramatist Lope de Vega (1562–1635). Here, as in other poems by Hill, religious and amorous imagery and themes are combined in allusive, unparaphrasable verse.

Jesse tree: a conventional way of representing the genealogy of Christ as a tree at whose base is Jesse and among whose boughs are his descendants.

TWO CHORALE-PRELUDES

Paul Celan (1920–70), the poet and translator, was born of Austrian Jews in Rumania as Paul Antschel. He lost his parents in the Nazi death-camps and was himself interned. Hill's poems take Celan's as points of departure. The musical motif is part and parcel of Hill's recent concerns as librettist, but allusions to music abound in his work.

Seamus Heaney

Seamus Heaney was born in County Londonderry, Northern Ireland, in 1939. He studied at the Queen's University, Belfast, and became a teacher. He reports that he began writing when he began teaching.

In the back of his mind are the rhythms and rhymes of the songs and chants of his childhood. His mature writing relates closely to the Irish world in which he grew up, and the Irish 'troubles' are an important theme in many of the poems which probe Irish history and prehistory and his own troubled conscience with considerable candour.

The particularity of the early poems which describe his own background earned wide applause when *Death Of A Naturalist* was published in 1966. Later collections include *Door Into The Dark* (1969), *Wintering Out* (1972), *North* (1975) and *Field Work* (1979).

Once he had exhausted the early vein, Heaney began to explore his Ireland through emblems of its past and, with travel, he gained a clearer perspective on the situation and on his place within it. The example of Patrick Kavanagh was important to him when he began. So too was that of R. S. Thomas. He learned much from his near-contemporaries.

Many of the early poems are vitiated by a kind of primitive trust in the force of onomatopoeia to bring over an experience or an image in sound. A partial reading of Hopkins must have contributed to the unsubtlety and to the labouredness of some of those early poems. Much of the art that Heaney has learned since comes from his reading of American and other contemporary poets. There is, too, a greater subtlety of organization in the later poems. Subtlety is not of itself a virtue, but neither is primitive plainness unless the poem is merely a simple evocation. Even in his earliest poems Heaney was after something more than mere evocation, and yet he had no other language but that rudimentary one. What is so impressive in his development is the assurance with which he has moved beyond the limited range of his early work.

Yet the early work is crucial to his whole vision. Born 'on the land', the eldest of eight children, he broke with his rural roots, trained academically and became a lecturer. His own career mirrors one of his social themes: the loss of 'the old traditional community which I knew as a child'. This loss is one of many. The movement away from 'traditional community' at first produces nostalgia and is therefore negative. Gradually the poetry, from book to book, gains in technical assurance and at the same time in thematic ambition. Heaney does not succumb to facile formulations, but there is in his verse a positive impulse even when his themes are negative. To recognize accurately the nature of a negative experience (as Hardy taught) is, even if remotely, a 'way to the better'. In identifying the historical nature of recurring ills – if not their source – he provides a valuable *civic* verse.

in respect of Ireland's troubles.

There is a strong element of celebration in Heaney's work as well, even if at times it is simply the celebration we associate with clear evocation.

Digging

Between my finger and my thumb
The squat pen rests; snug as a gun.

Under my window, a clean rasping sound
When the spade sinks into gravelly ground:
My father, digging. I look down

Till his straining rump among the flowerbeds
Bends low, comes up twenty years away *going back in time.*
Stooping in rhythm through potato drills
Where he was digging.

⌐ projection on an object.

The coarse boot nestled on the lug, the shaft
Against the inside knee was levered firmly.
He rooted out tall tops, buried the bright edge deep
To scatter new potatoes that we picked
Loving their cool hardness in our hands.

Sensual

By God, the old man could handle a spade.
Just like his old man.

My grandfather cut more turf in a day
Than any other man on Toner's bog.
Once I carried him milk in a bottle
Corked sloppily with paper. He straightened up
To drink it, then fell to right away
Nicking and slicing neatly, heaving sods   *Skill*
Over his shoulder, going down and down
For the good turf. Digging.

The cold smell of potato mould, the squelch and slap
Of soggy peat, the curt cuts of an edge
Through living roots awaken in my head. *acknowledging*
But I've no spade to follow men like them. *their importance*
Sense of shame   *to him*

Between my finger and my thumb
The squat pen rests.
I'll dig with it.

↳ learnt to acknowledge importance of past while living
separate from it.

The Diviner

Cut from the green hedge a forked hazel stick
That he held tight by the arms of the V:
Circling the terrain, hunting the pluck – *twitch / movement.*
Of water, nervous, but professionally
                    ie confident in job
Unfussed. The pluck came sharp as a sting.
The rod jerked down with precise convulsions,
Spring water suddenly broadcasting
Through a green aerial its secret stations.

The bystanders would ask to have a try.
He handed them the rod without a word.
It lay dead in their grasp till nonchalantly
He gripped expectant wrists. The hazel stirred.

Sense of a calling - somebody
picked out for a special job - not only
that - it is a job d instinct - one which one is naturally born to do.

(handwritten: mountain sacred to the Muses.)

Personal Helicon

For Michael Longley

As a child, they could not keep me from wells
And old pumps with buckets and windlasses. *(handwritten: machine for hoisting)*
I loved the dark drop, the trapped sky, the smells
Of waterweed, fungus and dank moss.

One, in a brickyard, with a rotted board top.
I savoured the rich crash when a bucket
Plummeted down at the end of a rope.
So deep you saw no reflection in it. *(handwritten: loss of self)*

(handwritten: each verse ends with the particular element & reflection - self.)

A shallow one under a dry stone ditch
Fructified like any aquarium. *(handwritten: more fruitful ie growth.)*
When you dragged out long roots from the soft mulch
A white face hovered over the bottom.

Others had echoes, gave back your own call
With a clean new music in it. And one
Was scaresome for there, out of ferns and tall
Foxgloves, a rat slapped across my reflection.

Now, to pry into roots, to finger slime,
To stare big-eyed Narcissus, into some spring
Is beneath all adult dignity. I rhyme
To see myself, to set the darkness echoing.

The Salmon Fisher to the Salmon

The ridged lip set upstream, you flail
Inland again, your exile in the sea
Unconditionally cancelled by the pull
Of your home water's gravity.

(handwritten: the fisher addressing the Salmon)

And I stand in the centre, casting.
The river cramming under me reflects
Slung gaff and net and a white wrist flicking
Flies well-dressed with tint and fleck.

(handwritten: type of fishing spear.)

209

author of the Compleat Angler.

ELEVEN BRITISH POETS

Walton thought garden worms, perfumed
By oil crushed from dark ivy berries
The lure that took you best, but here you come
    To grief through hunger in your eyes.

Ripples arrowing beyond me,
The current strumming water up my leg,
Involved in water's choreography
    I go, like you, by gleam and drag

And will strike when you strike, to kill.
We're both annihilated on the fly.
You can't resist a gullet full of steel.
    I will turn home fish-smelling, scaly.

both will go to kill at some time — this is how fishing works.

Sense of contamination through killing?

identifying himself with the fish.

The Forge

Sanctity + mystery of particular skills.

All I know is a door into the dark.
Outside, old axles and iron hoops rusting;
Inside, the hammered anvil's short-pitched ring, *perfect.*
The unpredictable fantail of sparks
Or hiss when a new shoe toughens in water.
The anvil must be somewhere in the centre,
Horned as a unicorn, at one end square,
Set there immoveable: an altar
like the poet. Where he expends himself in shape and music.
Sometimes, leather-aproned, hairs in his nose,
He leans out on the jamb, recalls a clatter
history — Of hoofs where traffic is flashing in rows;
Then grunts and goes in, with a slam and flick
To beat real iron out, to work the bellows.

Satisfaction in work.

The Peninsula

When you have nothing more to say, just drive
For a day all round the peninsula.
The sky is tall as over a runway,
The land without marks so you will not arrive

SEAMUS HEANEY

But pass through, though always skirting landfall.
At dusk, horizons drink down sea and hill,
The ploughed field swallows the whitewashed gable
And you're in the dark again. Now recall

The glazed foreshore and silhouetted log,
That rock where breakers shredded into rags,
The leggy birds stilted on their own legs,
Islands riding themselves out into the fog

Here nothing needs to be said – visual experience.

And drive back home, still with nothing to say
Except that now you will uncode all landscapes
By this: things founded clean on their own shapes,
Water and ground in their extremity.

Fodder

Or, as we said,
fother, I open
my arms for it
again. But first

open form
Influenced by W.C. Williams in short lines + in going over line endings.

good at time warps

to draw from the tight
vise of a stack
the weathered eaves
of the stack itself

falling at your feet,
last summer's tumbled
swathes of grass
and meadowsweet

multiple as loaves
and fishes, a bundle
tossed over half-doors
or into mucky gaps.

nourishing + comforting

These long nights
I would pull hay
for comfort, anything
to bed the stall.

symbol of home / what matters.

sense of emptiness.

211

Identifies with him as a symbol of hope.

Servant Boy

He is wintering out *Sense of endurance.*
the back-end of a bad year, *Sense of it coming to an*
swinging a hurricane-lamp *end, maybe*
through some outhouse;

a jobber among shadows.
Old work-whore, slave-
blood, who stepped fair-hills
under each bidder's eye

and kept your patience *le himself to himself.*
and your counsel, how
you draw me into *fascinated by him*
your trail. Your trail

on his trail into past + history + literally following his back — word play

broken from haggard to stable,
a straggle of fodder
stiffened on snow,
comes first-footing

He is Ireland, the 'little barons' are England?

the back doors of the little
barons: resentful
and impenitent,
carrying the warm eggs. *hope, life.*

Or more vaguely he is a symbol of endurance + with that, hope.

The Wool Trade

*'How different are the words "home",
"Christ", "ale", "master", on his
lips and on mine.'*
STEPHEN DEDALUS

'The wool trade' – the phrase
Rambled warm as a fleece

Out of his hoard.
To shear, to bale and bleach and card

Unwound from the spools
Of his vowels

And square-set men in tunics
Who plied soft names like Bruges

In their talk, merchants
Back from the Netherlands:

O all the hamlets where
Hills and flocks and streams conspired

To a language of waterwheels,
A lost syntax of looms and spindles,

How they hang
Fading, in the gallery of the tongue!

And I must talk of tweed,
A stiff cloth with flecks like blood.

[handwritten margin notes: "Wool - represents the warm, friendly, individual dialects" / "Tweed - sense d. uniform thy : cold, hard. Uniformity of accent?" / "the old country dialects - history / tradition." / "Ominous. This losing of the individual dialects / personalities will result in more bloodshed - resentment. Tweed - not natural, forced. Unlikeable."]

The Tollund Man

I

Some day I will go to Aarhus
To see his peat-brown head,
The mild pods of his eye-lids,
His pointed skin cap.

In the flat country nearby
Where they dug him out,
His last gruel of winter seeds
Caked in his stomach,

Naked except for
The cap, noose and girdle,
I will stand a long time.
Bridegroom to the goddess,

She tightened her torc on him *[le the goddess of the bog.]*
And opened her fen,
Those dark juices working
Him to a saint's kept body,

Trove of the turfcutters' *[treasure which they found.]*
Honeycombed workings.
Now his stained face
Reposes at Aarhus.

II

I could risk blasphemy,
Consecrate the cauldron bog
Our holy ground and pray
Him to make germinate

The scattered, ambushed
Flesh of labourers,
Stockinged corpses
Laid out in the farmyards,

Tell-tale skin and teeth
Flecking the sleepers
Of four young brothers, trailed
For miles along the lines.

III

Something of his sad freedom
As he rode the tumbril *[open cart]*
Should come to me, driving,
Saying the names

Tollund, Grabaulle, Nebelgard,
Watching the pointing hands
Of country people,
Not knowing their tongue.

Out there in Jutland
In the old man-killing parishes
I will feel lost,
Unhappy and at home.

May

When I looked down from the bridge
Trout were flipping the sky
Into smithereens, the stones
Of the wall warmed me.

Wading green stems, lugs of leaf
That untangle and bruise
(Their tiny gushers of juice)
My toecaps sparkle now

Over the soft fontanel *membrane in infant's skull - soft spot?*
Of Ireland. I should wear
Hide shoes, the hair next my skin,
For walking this ground: *to be gentle upon it.*

Wasn't there a spa-well,
Its coping grassy, pendent?
And then the spring issuing *breaking free over a man made*
Right across the tarmac. *surface.*

I'm out to find that village, *does it exist, or a nostalgic*
Its low sills fragrant *figment of his*
With ladysmock and celandine, *imagination?*
Marshlights in the summer dark.

Westering

In California

I sit under Rand McNally's
'Official Map of the Moon' –
The colour of frogskin,
Its enlarged pores held

Open and one called
'Pitiscus' at eye level –
Recalling the last night
In Donegal, my shadow

Neat upon the whitewash
From her bony shine,
The cobbles of the yard
Lit pale as eggs.

Summer had been a free fall
Ending there,
The empty amphitheatre
Of the west. Good Friday

We had started out
Past shopblinds drawn on the afternoon,
Cars stilled outside still churches,
Bikes tilting to a wall;

We drove by,
A dwindling interruption
As clappers smacked
On a bare altar

And congregations bent
To the studded crucifix.
What nails dropped out that hour?
Roads unreeled, unreeled

Falling light as casts
Laid down
On shining waters.
Under the moon's stigmata

Six thousand miles away,
I imagine untroubled dust,
A loosening gravity,
Christ weighing by his hands.

216

Mossbawn: Two Poems in Dedication

For Mary Heaney

1 *Sunlight*

There was a sunlit absence.
The helmeted pump in the yard
heated its iron,
water honeyed

in the slung bucket
and the sun stood
like a griddle cooling
against the wall

of each long afternoon.
So, her hands scuffled
over the bakeboard,
the reddening stove

sent its plaque of heat
against her where she stood
in a floury apron
by the window.

Now she dusts the board
with a goose's wing,
now sits, broad-lapped,
with whitened nails

and measling shins:
here is a space
again, the scone rising
to the tick of two clocks.

And here is love
like a tinsmith's scoop
sunk past its gleam
in the meal-bin.

love as something deep and real you can dig down into.

217

2 *The Seed Cutters*

They seem hundreds of years away. Breughel,
You'll know them if I can get them true.
They kneel under the hedge in a half-circle
Behind a windbreak wind is breaking through.
They are the seed cutters. The tuck and frill
Of leaf-sprout is on the seed potatoes
Buried under that straw. With time to kill
They are taking their time. Each sharp knife goes
Lazily halving each root that falls apart
In the palm of the hand: a milky gleam,
And, at the centre, a dark watermark.
O calendar customs! Under the broom
Yellowing over them, compose the frieze
With all of us there, our anonymities.

Identifying self through seasonal / agricultural activities

Punishment

I can feel the tug
of the halter at the nape
of her neck, the wind
on her naked front.

It blows her nipples
to amber beads,
it shakes the frail rigging
of her ribs.

I can see her drowned
body in the bog,
the weighing stone,
the floating rods and boughs.

Under which at first
she was a barked sapling
that is dug up
oak-bone, brain-firkin:

her shaved head
like a stubble of black corn,
her blindfold a soiled bandage,
her noose a ring

to store
the memories of love.
Little adulteress,
before they punished you

you were flaxen-haired,
undernourished, and your
tar-black face was beautiful.
My poor scapegoat,

I almost love you
but would have cast, I know,
the stones of silence.
I am the artful voyeur

of your brain's exposed
and darkened combs,
your muscles' webbing
and all your numbered bones:

I who have stood dumb
when your betraying sisters,
cauled in tar,
wept by the railings,

who would connive
in civilized outrage
yet understand the exact
and tribal, intimate revenge.

Exposure

It is December in Wicklow:
Alders dripping, birches
Inheriting the last light,
The ash tree cold to look at.

A comet that was lost
Should be visible at sunset,
Those million tons of light
Like a glimmer of haws and rose-hips,

219

And I sometimes see a falling star.
If I could come on meteorite!
Instead I walk through damp leaves, ↓ bathos
Husks, the spent flukes of autumn,

Imagining a hero
On some muddy compound,
His gift like a slingstone
Whirled for the desperate.

How did I end up like this?
I often think of my friends'
Beautiful prismatic counselling
And the anvil brains of some who hate me

He has escaped physically + he feels he has failed poetically

As I sit weighing and weighing
My responsible *tristia*.
For what? For the ear? For the people?
For what is said behind-backs?

Rain comes down through the alders,
Its low conducive voices
Mutter about let-downs and erosions
And yet each drop recalls

The diamond absolutes. *the ideals he used to have.*
I am neither internee nor informer; *outside, on the fence.*
An inner émigré, grown long-haired
And thoughtful; a wood-kerne

He has escaped, but in doing so has missed out on something great.

Escaped from the massacre,
Taking protective colouring   *— protecting him from others.*
From bole and bark, feeling
Every wind that blows; — *but not from himself.*

Who, blowing up these sparks
For their meagre heat, have missed
The once-in-a-lifetime portent,
The comet's pulsing rose.

To whom should he show loyalty — himself and his family or his country?

After a Killing

There they were, as if our memory hatched them,
As if the unquiet founders walked again: *Circularity of history*
Two young men with rifles on the hill,
Profane and bracing as their instruments.

Who's sorry for our trouble?
Who dreamt that we might dwell among ourselves
In rain and scoured light and wind-dried stones?
Basalt, blood, water, headstones, leeches.

In that neuter original loneliness
From Brandon to Dunseverick   *refuge in nature?*
I think of small-eyed survivor flowers,
The pined-for, unmolested orchid.

I see a stone house by a pier.
Elbow room. Broad window light.   *purity +*
The heart lifts. You walk twenty yards   *goodness.*
To the boats and buy mackerel.   *Get back to the*
                                            land/ romantic
And to-day a girl walks in home to us   *Sense it as a*
Carrying a basket full of new potatoes,   *refuge rather*
Three tight green cabbages, and carrots   *than a solution?*
With the tops and mould still fresh on them.

Leavings

A soft whoosh, the sunset blaze
of straw on blackened stubble,
a thatch-deep, freshening
barbarous crimson burn –

I rode down England
as they fired the crop
that was the leavings of a crop,
the smashed tow-coloured barley,

very right

221

down from Ely's Lady Chapel,
the sweet tenor latin
forever banished,
the sumptuous windows

threshed clear by Thomas Cromwell.
Which circle does he tread, *[handwritten: ie in hell - punishment.]*
scalding on cobbles,
each one a broken statue's head? *[handwritten: ie from the buildings he had demolished]*

[handwritten left margin: all endings, images of destruction ↓ but turns in the end to a positive image.]

After midnight, after summer,
to walk in a sparking field,
to smell dew and ashes
and start Will Brangwen's ghost

from the hot soot –
a breaking sheaf of light,
abroad in the hiss
and clash of stooking. *[handwritten: arranging in stooks.]*

NOTES

PERSONAL HELICON

Helicon, a Boeotian mountain sacred to the Muses, is where the springs of Helicon and Aganippe flow. Heaney seems to have confused or conflated the mountain with the springs.

THE SALMON FISHER TO THE SALMON

Walton: Izaac Walton (1593–1683), author of *The Compleat Angler* (1653, 1655).

THE WOOL TRADE

Stephen Dedalus: the protagonist of James Joyce's *A Portrait of the Artist as a Young Man* and a character in *Ulysses*.

THE TOLLUND MAN

This refers to an almost perfectly preserved Iron Age corpse discovered in a Danish peat-bog in 1950. He had been hanged. His last meal could be analysed by scientists. The head is displayed in a museum in Aarhus.

WESTERING

Rand McNally: publishers of maps and atlases in the United States.

MOSSBAWN: THE SEED CUTTERS

Breughel: Peter Breughel, sixteenth-century Dutch painter whose portrayals of peasants labouring, at rest and at play are vivid in their particularity.

PUNISHMENT

firkin: a small cask for liquids, etc.

EXPOSURE

This is part six of the autobiographical sequence 'Singing School' from *North*.

   tristia: sad or melancholy thoughts.

AFTER A KILLING

This is the first part of the sequence 'Triptych'.

LEAVINGS

This poem, like many in Heaney's collection *Field Work*, is pervaded by Dante's *Divine Comedy*, with the circles of Hell and Purgatory where sinners are sent for their rewards.

   Thomas Cromwell: (1485?–1540) Henry VIII's chief adviser in ecclesiastical matters, principal promoter of the dissolution of the monasteries.

   Will Brangwen: see D. H. Lawrence, *The Rainbow*.

Index of first lines

A cool small evening shrunk to a dog bark and the clank of a bucket 177
After the fiesta, the beauty-contests, the drunken wrestling 181
Against the burly air I strode, 186
Alistair approach this thirty 54
A little ash, a painted rose, a name. 139
All I know is a door into the dark. 210
All plants grow here; the most minute, 157
'All strangers now; there is nobody that I know.' 27
All travellers escape the mainland here. 114
A long house – 137
Always too eager for the future, we 96
And having built it 20
And he is an owl 177
And I standing in the shade 18
And it may be that we have no nature 31
And the word came – was it a god 22
Another time, this way the primrose, 37
An owl's call scrapes the stillness. 120
A poem is less an orange than a grid; 71
Arable acres heave 81
Arden is not Eden, but Eden's rhyme: 142
Are you to say goodnight 64
As a child, they could not keep me from wells 209
A shrunken world 83
A soft whoosh, the sunset blaze 221
As when a ruined face 85
A way of many ways: a god 189
A word for everybody, myself nobody, 46
Between my finger and my thumb 207

Beyond all this, the wish to be alone: 97
Burning 181
Closed like confessionals, they thread 105
Comes home dull with coal-dust deliberately 174
Coming home was to that: 13
Coming up England by a different line 99
Convergences 19
Crow saw the herded mountains, steaming in the morning. 179
Cut from the green hedge a forked hazel stick 208
Deep-sea frost, and 79
Downtown, an office tower is going up. 158
For nations vague as weed, 103
Four people in a street where houses were 121
Gold is not autumn's privilege; 75
Groping back to bed after a piss 110
Hearing one saga, we enact the next. 72
He is the watcher underneath the stars. 125
He is wintering out 212
He ran the course and as he ran he grew, 152
Her father's brother rapes her! 86
He will go over and tell the king 39
How distant, the departure of young men 109
How to speak with the dead 138
Hunger was loneliness, betrayed 14
Iago Prytherch his name, though, be it allowed, 10
I am a man now. 15
I called today, Peter, and you were away. 57
I can feel the tug 218
I climbed through woods in the hour-before-dawn dark. 167
I do not want to pour my heart out any more 38
I feel I could be turned to ice 122
If I could only find a little stream 42
I had forgotten 21
I have been all men known to history, 12
I have come into the hour of a white healing. 123
I have grown wary of the ways of love 125
I have seen it standing up grey, 16
I imagine this midnight moment's forest: 165
I leave you in your garden. 150
I love my work and my children. God 191
Imagine a forest 59
In darkness I set out, 32
In reply to your last letter 56
Inside the room I see the table laid, 116

I sit in the top of the wood, my eyes closed. 171
I sit under Rand McNally's 215
I smell a smell of death. 81
It does not matter how are you how are 64
I think of a man on foot 159
It is a quality of air, a temperate sharpness 130
It is December in Wicklow: 219
It is not life being short, 82
It is the evening brought me here, 43
It was a language of water, light and air 139
It was a time when wise men 19
It was a violent time. Wheels, racks, and fires 147
It was like a church to me. 16
I understand you well enough, John Donne 28
I was the dweller in the long cave 14
I was the one who waited in the garden 119
I will consider the outnumbering dead: 188
Last night I saw the savage world 118
Let it disturb no more at first 117
Let me measure my prayer with sleep as an 53
Let there be treaties, bridges, 136
Lighting a spill late in the afternoon, 76
Listen. Put on morning. 55
My father sat in his chair recovering 175
My life is given over to follies 28
Never the same and all again. 126
Northward I came, and knocked in the coated wall 80
Not as in the old days I pray, 20
Not forgetting Ko-jen, that 130
Not that he brought flowers 17
No trellisses, no vines 158
Now the river is rich, but her voice is low. 182
October is marigold, and yet 169
Often I try 17
O gentle queen of the afternoon 52
Once I am sure there's nothing going on 98
One by one they appear in 153
On the day of the explosion 111
Or, as we said, 211
Out of my window late at night I gape 115
O will you take a fluttering swan 30
Portland, the Isle of Portland – how I love 85
Prodigal of loves and barbecues, 190
Scarcely a street, too few houses 12

She kept an antique shop – or it kept her.   118
Side by side, their faces blurred,   106
Sleep has my muscles and a cord my throat.   34
So many nights the solitary lamp had burned;   84
Some day I will go to Aarhus   213
Some days a shadow through   192
Something is taking place.   156
So that each person may quickly find that   61
So they came   120
Still with the hope of being understood,   37
Such a fool as I am you had better ignore   35
Summer thunder darkens, and its climbing   135
Swerving east, from rich industrial shadows   101
Swimming the horses at Appleby in Westmorland   41
Ten years without you. For so it happens.   194
Terrifying are the attent sleek thrushes on the lawn,   173
That firewood pale with salt and burning green   54
The apes yawn and adore their fleas in the sun.   166
The blue jay scuffling in the bushes follows   148
The celluloid of a photograph holds them well, –   170
The day goes slowly, it is the first day   41
The eye can hardly pick them out   100
The light of the mind is poorer   138
The pig lay on a barrow dead.   172
The plunging year, the bright year. Through the clouds   45
The sniff of the real, that's   160
There are portraits and still-lives.   129
There is a heigh-ho in these glowing coals   76
There is a land called Lost   202
There is an evening coming in   97
There is an island there is no going   23
There they were, as if our memory hatched them,   221
There was a sunlit absence.   217
The ridged lip set upstream, you flail   209
The Schmidts obeyed, and marched on Poland.   155
These claws too contain   124
These I have set up,   74
The snail pushes through a green   152
The un-red deer   27
The wind blew all my wedding-day,   95
The wings tremble, it is the red admiral   44
'The wool trade' – the phrase   212
They are fencing the upland against   132
They slew by night   196

This house has been far out at sea all night, 168
This is pain's landscape. 18
'This was Mr Bleaney's room. He stayed 102
Those houses haunt in which we leave 115
Time passing, and the memories of love 74
Today, should you let fall a glass it would 128
To live in Wales is to be conscious 11
To one kneeling down no word came, 12
To touch was an accord 121
Undesirable you may have been, untouchable 191
Waiting for when the sun an hour or less 151
Walking around in the park 104
What am I? Nosing here, turning leaves over 178
What are days for? 105
What do they think has happened, the old fools, 107
What is the person? Is it hope? 34
What night, corrupt, as this must be, with dreams 38
What should one 131
When I looked down from the bridge 215
When I see a couple of kids 109
When I was a child and the soft flesh was forming 11
When the eagle soared clear through a dawn distilling of emerald 180
When you have nothing more to say, just drive 210
Whereas I wander here among 26
Where the living with effort go, 188
Who are they talking to in the big temple? 27
Who is the man that stands against this bridge 141
Who owns these scrawny little feet? *Death*. 179
Why, by an ingrained habit, elevate 77
Winter will bar the swimmer soon. 134
You are already 154
You are confronted with yourself. Each year 122
Your neighbour moves less and less, attempts less. 174
You who would have me often cynical 124